D1015874

Vegetarian Heartland

Vegetarian Heartland

RECIPES FOR LIFE'S ADVENTURES

Shelly Westerhausen

CHRONICLE BOOKS
SAN FRANCISCO

Text and photographs copyright © 2017 by Shelly Westerhausen.

Library of Congress Cataloging-in-Publication Data

Names: Westerhausen, Shelly, author.
Title: Vegetarian heartland : recipes for life's adventures /
    Shelly Westerhausen.
Description: San Francisco : Chronicle Books, [2016] |
    Includes index.
Identifiers: LCCN 2016019917 | ISBN 9781452154701
    (hc : alk. paper)
Subjects: LCSH: Cooking, American—Midwestern style. |
    Vegetarian cooking. | LCGFT: Cookbooks.
Classification: LCC TX715.2.M53 W47 2016 |
    DDC 641.5/636—dc23 LC record available at
    https://lccn.loc.gov/2016019917

Manufactured in China

Designed by Alice Chau

Prop and food styling by Shelly Westerhausen

Illustrations on page 166 by Keara McGraw

Chronicle books and gifts are available at special quantity discounts to corporations, professional associations, literacy programs, and other organizations. For details and discount information, please contact our premiums department at corporatesales@chroniclebooks.com or at 1-800-759-0190.

10 9 8 7 6 5 4 3 2 1

Chronicle Books LLC
680 Second Street
San Francisco, California 94107
www.chroniclebooks.com

To Oma Betty Fry for always being my biggest fan and for encouraging me to never stop reading, writing, and learning.

introduction

This cookbook might have caught your eye because you're considering becoming a vegetarian. Or maybe you are already committed to a plant-based diet, for many of the beneficial reasons for not eating meat. It could be that you picked up this cookbook because you are incorporating more vegetables into your meals upon your doctor's suggestion and realize that you don't have to sacrifice delicious, flavorful food. Maybe you love meat and have no plans of abandoning it but want to shake up your culinary routine. Maybe you're a seasoned vegetarian and are excited to continue discovering new plant-based recipes.

Whatever drew you to pick it up, this book is about delicious food, the joy of eating with a conscience, uncomplicated recipes, and mouth-watering photographs. My intention with my recipes is to put a twist on the classics, adding a hint of the unknown by swapping in new flavors and fresh, whole-food ingredients.

I came to vegetarianism early, purely because of animal rights, when I stopped eating meat at age twelve. I also started to love cooking and cookbooks at a young age, fascinated with a Mickey Mouse cookbook that belonged to my babysitter. I would flip through its pages, feeling a creative sensation running through my body, realizing I could make something delicious simply by following the steps of a recipe! She eventually gave me that book, and it still holds a space among the cookbooks on my bookshelf today.

Becoming a vegetarian was almost unheard of in my small northern Indiana town during the early 2000s. My father stocked our upright freezer with a side of beef purchased from the farmer down the street, and the closest thing we had to a vegetarian restaurant was an Italian place that served a few meat-free pasta entrées. Although she tried her hardest, my supportive mother had trouble finding creative ways to feed me. It was before our town had a large bookstore that carried magazines or cookbooks, and also before the Internet became a bottomless source for recipes.

I lived on pasta and peanut butter and jelly for the first few years, until I discovered I could take control of what I was eating by making my own meals. Most of the recipes I found contained meat, so I began to alter them by swapping in beans or leaving the meat out. I didn't realize it at the time, but these were my first attempts at recipe developing; although they weren't all successful, they sure were exciting, and they were the starting point for my love of cooking!

When I was old enough to take the train into Chicago, I'd spend Saturdays hanging out with friends in the city. We'd head there to see a concert, but we'd arrive hours early to explore a culture much richer than that in our small suburban town. Restaurant menus had vegetarian options! We went to the Chicago Diner, the famous Chicago vegetarian spot known for serving diner style food without the meat. At home, I'd then try to re-create the recipes in my kitchen.

At college in gorgeous Bloomington, Indiana, I discovered ethnic food and natural grocery stores. Initially, I was overwhelmed with all the options. But I was also so excited about the potential of learning so many new vegetarian techniques that I started my food blog, *Vegetarian 'Ventures*, to record my discoveries and adventures in the kitchen. Early on, there were as many failures as successes in my kitchen, which I openly talked about on my blog, but these only pushed me to try harder. As I became more comfortable, I began to rely less on processed meat replacements and more on beans and whole grains for protein. And years later, I've come to appreciate my vegetarian diet even more for its health benefits and reduced environmental impact.

Another amazing resource in Bloomington is the farmers' market. Relying on this weekly market for picking meals based on what's available taught me to eat seasonally and locally. Learning to navigate the seasons and all they have to offer opened up endless options in the kitchen. I starting making seasonal variations on classic recipes as well as new recipes based on produce I wouldn't normally find in the grocery store (morels! ramps! black garlic!).

Jump to the present and vegetarian restaurants are as common as coffee shops. The term *vegetarian* has become a buzzword among Americans looking for a more healthful lifestyle. I love the accessibility of vegetarian cuisine in this day and age, but the Midwest still has a long way to go. When not in larger Midwest cities, it can still be a struggle to find healthful meat-free cuisine. Learning to rely on your own cooking skills has become essential for all heartland vegetarians.

I hope this book will become a resource for everyone (not only Midwesterners!) looking to introduce more creative, satisfying vegetarian dishes to their repertoire. For all of us who live in the Midwest, this book is a special resource for you, as I've focused on the fresh, local produce our climate, fertile soil, and wide-open spaces yield year-round. It's time to cook with all of the freshly picked vegetables, local dairy farm products, and organic grains from the breadbasket we live in, so seek out those resources and create some delicious and nutritious meals with all our land has to offer!

ON MY ADVENTURE CHAPTERS

Do you remember the first road trip you ever took with friends? Or the first time you plunged headfirst into a complicated recipe to cook for your significant other? What about the day you brought your pet home from the shelter, or the moment you felt so small gazing across the Great Lakes? When was the last time you slept in the woods under the night skies or felt that overwhelming, cleansing feeling after jumping into a cold lake?

Adventures come in all shapes and sizes, and I consider it an adventure anytime you jump into the unknown with all senses firing. Sometimes cooking can be an adventure—walk into your kitchen and put together new flavors, follow a new recipe, try out an unknown vegetable, or develop a new cooking technique. I'm here to

encourage vegetarian adventures in your own kitchen.

Because I live by my sense of adventure in all things, the recipes in this book are organized into adventures specific to each season. The categories follow the kinds of exploring I like to do in my region, but the food works for all kinds of outings. For example, the Peanut Butter Trail Mix Cookies (page 192) found in the hiking section are also great for road trips, camping, or even an afternoon snack at school or work. The Whole-Wheat Pumpkin & Poppy Seed Crackers (page 50) are not only perfect for picnics but also for holiday hosting and road trips.

It's easy to walk into a restaurant and eat a pleasant lunch or run into a café to grab a sandwich to eat on the way to your next destination. But, for me, a big part about making my own meals is cooking with intention—I don't just enjoy what I'm eating, but I enjoy the process of preparing it, too. I structured the book by adventure themes because I want it to be an experience every time you step into your kitchen. Your food should feel like a welcome part of your routine instead of a nuisance wedged among the rest of your daily tasks. Many of the chapters that follow are about the food that you can bring along with you on your adventures, but I like to think of the whole process of cooking, starting with picking out your ingredients, as the adventure.

Creating engaging memories with your food is also a way to get you more excited about planning your future meals. Let's be real: are you more likely to get excited about that breakfast sandwich grabbed from the convenience store or about the breakfast bake that you prepped the night before and baked for a few friends before a busy workday? Not every day is going to allow time for these slow moments, but planning ahead will make them more likely to happen. Enjoy these recipes on the go when necessary but also make sure to set some time aside to really enjoy them at home when you can.

THE MIDWEST

The Midwest is my home, and I honestly cannot imagine living without four seasons or the Great Lakes nearby. Most of my friends from high school and college have all gravitated toward the coasts. After graduating from Indiana University, my boyfriend and I visited a handful of cities across the country, but during these trips, we missed Bloomington dearly and were happy to return to it. We visited the creative communities in New York and Portland and explored the amazing food scenes in Austin and San Francisco but found ourselves comparing them to the tightly knit creative community and streets of restaurants dedicated to world cuisine in Bloomington. We realized we were searching for a home in a big American city because it was expected of us as young, creative entrepreneurs but soon realized Bloomington already had everything we need and want.

A good friend from Indiana, who now lives in New York City, once said that he thinks the Midwest has "self-esteem issues." That line really stuck with me; I noticed it more and more as I chatted with friends so eager to get out of the Midwest that they were missing all of the wonderful things the heartland offers. Maybe they took for granted the seasonal produce, engaging art scenes, and expansive landscapes. The Midwest is oftentimes overlooked because people see its vast, wide-open farming fields and immediately conjure up the word *lacking*, but that lacking is being confused for our unique open space that lets you see for miles on end. Driving through endless open fields, where you can oftentimes go for long stretches without running into another car, can be as freeing as hiking a mountaintop. You can find your own space on the sandy beaches of Lake Michigan because it's rarely overcrowded, and when it's too cold to venture outside, there's the comfort of a cozy afternoon spent indoors baking to warm the house.

Our heartland has gorgeous beaches, waterfalls, cliffs, fishing towns, lighthouses, caves, art galleries, music scenes, and award-winning restaurants, but they are sometimes overlooked because of the miles and miles of farmland that divides them all. I hope this book inspires you to get into your kitchen to create delicious, vegetarian recipes and also take those meals on adventures. Find the overlooked gems, either in the Midwest or in your own area. It's gorgeous out there—go explore it!

Stocking a Vegetarian Pantry

This chapter is dedicated to stocking your pantry for a diet with lots of protein but no meat. The average amount of protein a human needs varies from person to person, but it's recommended that you consume between 46 and 56 grams per day. Meeting these requirements should be no problem if you are eating a varied diet, including legumes, nuts, milk, cheese, leafy greens, and whole grains.

Cheese: When I talk to people about being a vegetarian, they are most often surprised by my self-imposed cheese restrictions. Not all cheeses are vegetarian. Many cheeses are made with animal rennet (enzymes derived from the stomach lining of cows, goats, sheep, and pigs) and should be avoided if you are trying to stick to a purely vegetarian diet. Luckily, a huge demand for vegetarian cheeses has sparked the attention of large companies, which are starting to label vegetarian cheeses. For example, in all of my recipes that call for Parmesan, I've used Organic Valley's shredded Parmesan. Other widely distributed brands such as BelGioioso also make a vegetarian Parmesan. If you pick up a cheese that you aren't sure about, try to find something on the label that indicates if it's vegetarian or ask the shop's cheese expert. Another option is to get your cheese from the farmers' market, where you can ask the dairy farmer directly how the cheese is made (you can even ask about the animals' living conditions if you choose). You can also swap in vegan "cheeses" for most of the recipes in this book; I'm a huge fan of Kite Hill because it's made from whole-food ingredients like nuts, and Daiya is sold at most national grocery stores. There are also a few recipes in this book for homemade nut cheeses (pages 53 and 259) if you'd like to make your own.

Butter, oils, and other fats: I use organic unsalted butter and olive oil because I have a great local source for both and feel good about the products I purchase. For the majority of these recipes, you can swap out butter with ghee, vegan butter (such as Earth Balance), or neutral oils (olive and coconut oils for low- or medium-heat cooking; peanut and sunflower oils for high heat). There are all sorts of guides for oils online and the facts in them vary greatly, so I often take the information in them lightly and just use what feels right to me. The most important thing to consider when deciding on an oil or fat is to choose the highest quality you possibly can. This means, if sticking with butter, purchase organic or local butter. If going with canola oil, make sure you choose a non-GMO or organic variety, as canola oil oftentimes gets a bad rap because of the heavy chemicals that may be sprayed on the rapeseed, the main plant ingredient in canola oil. Coconut oil is many people's choice for its numerous health benefits but should be avoided if you have heart issues. Coconut oil comes in solid form, but I oftentimes call for melted coconut oil in recipes; it melts at 76°F (24°C). Just as with melting butter for a recipe, you can scoop the solid coconut oil into a pan, heat it just enough to melt, and then measure out how much your recipe has called for. We don't do much frying in this book, but if we did, then it would be the right time to pull out the peanut or sunflower oil.

Salt: These recipes include salt measurements that you should consider as guidelines, keeping in mind that everyone prefers a different amount of seasoning. If possible, I'd recommend using fine sea salt in these recipes as it is full of nutrient-dense minerals and is also what I used when developing these recipes. Taste and add more or less salt as you prefer. With this in mind, I've tried to give the minimum amount I'd want to use. Consider adding more at the end, if needed.

KEEPING YOUR PANTRY STOCKED ON A BUDGET

Using fresh and local ingredients is key when making vegetarian cuisine. Buying local and organic can sometimes get expensive, but you will taste the difference, since the flavors of high-quality produce really shine in vegetarian dishes. Here are a few money-saving tips that will help mitigate the higher prices you pay for fresh produce.

Use dried beans. Buying dried beans in bulk oftentimes costs just one-tenth of buying canned. Cooking with dried beans is easy; just make sure you plan ahead and soak the beans the night before. I usually soak chickpeas and black beans on Saturday nights and cook a big batch of each on Sunday to keep me stocked for the week. If you make too many beans, you can also freeze them for later! (See page 264.)

Don't throw away vegetable peels and other trimmings. Instead, save them in a resealable plastic bag in the freezer. Once the bag is full, throw the trimmings into a big pot with a few spices of your choosing (I usually do whole peppercorns and a bay leaf), fill the pot with water, and boil for 1 hour. Strain by pouring through a fine-mesh sieve, discarding the scraps and—voilà!—you have vegetable stock! (See page 254 for a more-detailed recipe.) Store, refrigerated, for up to 5 days or freeze for up to 3 months in ice-cube trays for easy access.

Buy local and in season. Produce that didn't have to be shipped from across the globe is going to cost less to get into your cart and the retailer is going to charge you less for it. Local produce is also fresher than food that traveled across the country.

Go to a farmers' market. Buying produce straight from the source is often the cheapest route, and you can be sure it is the freshest you can find (aside from growing it yourself). This is also a great way to meet your local farmers and learn where your vegetables come from.

Plant a garden! Whether it is a small potted herb garden on your windowsill or a huge back-yard vegetable garden, every little bit of cultivated soil counts. Growing your own vegetables, fruits, or herbs gives you control of what is sprayed on your food, what you have access to, and an appreciation for all the work that goes into creating food from seed.

Buy specialty ingredients in bulk. If using an ingredient that isn't a staple in your kitchen, buy just the amount you need to avoid wasting the rest.

Stock your pantry with flavor boosters.
Vegetable-based cooking should never be bland or leave you wanting something else afterward. Vegetarian cuisine relies less on fat for flavor than the typical American diet and instead leans on seasoning and spices to lend bold flavors. Here are a few of my favorite flavor boosters:

» **Black pepper:** I use freshly ground black pepper in all the recipes in this book and encourage you to do the same (or plan to add more pepper than the recipe calls for if you are using preground pepper, which loses its flavor over time). As black peppercorns are already a staple in most kitchens, I recommend investing in a pepper mill so that pepper can always be freshly ground.

» **Chipotle peppers in adobo sauce:** These little peppers—smoked jalapeños in a thick sauce—pack a ton of flavor and burst with heat and smokiness. To use, pull out one or two at a time and finely dice with 1 tsp or so of the sauce. I recommend freezing the remaining chiles in a resealable plastic bag with parchment paper between each chile so you can pull out as needed.

» **Dijon mustard:** This mustard adds a sharp tang to any dish and is readily available at grocery stores. Keep it on hand not only as a condiment but to throw into recipes for a flavor boost as well.

» **Dried fruit:** Adding an accent of dried fruit (raisins, cranberries, apricots) brings the perfect sweet-tart touch to many savory dishes and adds a chewy texture and a pop of color. Since the flavor of dried fruit is concentrated, always start with just a little in a dish and add more as needed.

» **Herbs:** Using fresh herbs guarantees a fresher-tasting end result that will mostly likely be more nutritious and flavorful. Buying fresh herbs can get expensive, so I recommend cultivating a little summer herb garden in your backyard or on your kitchen windowsill. Herbs are a great way to get familiar with growing your own food because they are so easy to cultivate; start with three to five herbs that you cook with the most and try to expand your garden a little each year. You'll find the majority of fresh herb-heavy recipes in this book are in the spring and summer chapters, so you can lean on your herb garden. In winter, I use dried herbs only when the herbs are not center stage.

» **Lemon juice:** A little squirt of lemon juice can elevate a dish from just okay to down-right amazing. Lemon juice not only adds a bright tang but also brings out all the other flavors of the dish to make everything taste brighter. Lemons last 2 to 3 weeks in the refrigerator, so I always buy a big bag of them to have on hand at all times. You never know when your dish is going to need an extra squirt of juice to bring its flavor to the next level.

» **Liquid smoke:** If you don't already follow a meat-free diet, than this ingredient may not be on your radar yet. This condiment adds a smoky flavor to any dish without ever having to pull out your grill. It is inexpensive and can be found in the condiments section of almost any grocery store. A little goes a long way, so start with 1 tsp and add more as needed, tasting all the while.

» **Maple syrup:** When a dish needs a touch of sweetness, maple syrup is my go-to. It can easily be stirred into a dish or drizzled on top. I use the Dark Color and Robust Flavor designated syrup (formerly called grade B) for all the recipes in this book, as it is rich in flavor, nutritious, and less refined.

» **Miso:** This paste is an umami flavor booster with huge nutritional benefits. I use white miso for all recipes that call for miso in this book, but red miso is also an option. If using red miso, keep in mind that it is not as sweet as white miso, so consider adding a bit of a sweetener, like maple syrup or honey, at the end, if needed.

» **Nutritional yeast:** Another ingredient that is highly prized in the vegan and vegetarian community is nutritional yeast. It's a yellow flake or powdered yeast that has a flavor best described as creamy and nutty; this makes it the perfect substitute for cheese in many dishes. It can be sprinkled on top of a dish or mixed in for an extra "cheesy" boost.

» **Smoked paprika:** Another way to add a smoky accent to a dish is to add smoked paprika. I keep both sweet and smoked paprikas in my pantry at all times because they yield different flavors. Paprika is a great spice for marinades and soups because its flavor is versatile and distinct without overpowering the other key flavors in a dish.

» **Tamari or soy sauce:** You may be surprised to find that these two ingredients appear in many non-Asian dishes in this book, but they are perfect for infusing some umami into a dish and helping intensify the other ingredients. I use tamari for all dishes in which tamari or soy sauce are called for because it has less sodium than soy sauce. Since tamari might not be common in all towns, I give the option to use soy sauce instead. Just note that soy sauce tends to be a bit saltier, so you may need to cut back on the amount of salt in the rest of the recipe. These are ingredients I always buy organic since a large amount of soybean products here in the United States are made from genetically modified seeds.

» **Vinegars:** Similar to using lemon juice, adding an acidic ingredient such as apple cider, red wine, balsamic, and rice vinegar will brighten a dish and bring out the featured flavors. There are tons of vinegars, so try out an array of them until you find out which ones work best for you. Apple cider vinegar is very popular in vegan cuisine, but my personal favorite is red wine vinegar. The flavor of red wine vinegar is a bit milder, and it works as an all-purpose vinegar in almost any recipe.

EQUATION FOR CREATING A VEGETARIAN MEAL

Another great way to stay within a budget is to make sure you are using up all of your produce before it goes bad. At least once a week, I'll throw together a meal based purely on what I have on hand. To use up leftover veggies, throw them into a frittata, roast them to top pasta, or make a vegetable bowl out of them.

Here is a loose guideline of how I build a meal out of what I have already stocked in my kitchen:

» Choose a base such as cooked grains, pasta, quinoa, or bread.

» Top with vegetables (steamed, roasted, raw, boiled, sautéed, and so on).

» Add a protein such as beans, eggs, toasted nuts, tofu, seitan, tempeh.

» Mix in flavor boosters: think herbs, lemon, oils, dressings, and many of the spices mentioned previously.

» Keep it simple: try not to mix too many flavor combinations, as they may get lost in translation.

Here are a few of my favorite combinations:

» Cooked Wheat Berries + Sautéed Diced Onions and Bell Peppers + Roasted Chickpeas + Balsamic Vinegar + Olive Oil

» Cooked Quinoa + Roasted Broccoli + Peanut Sauce (page 56) + Toasted Sesame Seeds

» Boiled Pasta or Gnocchi + Blanched Peas and Asparagus + Lemon Zest + Olive Oil + Toasted Pine Nuts

» Bed of Cooked Millet + Roasted Sweet Potatoes, Tempeh, and Onion Wedges + Caramelized Date Barbecue Sauce (page 262)

» Cooked Brown Rice + Cooked Black Beans (see page 264 for how to cook beans in a slow cooker) + Sautéed Potatoes, Bell Peppers, and Red Onions + Homemade Enchilada Sauce (page 263)

» Cooked Polenta + Fried Egg + Sautéed Spinach and Garlic + Freshly Ground Pepper

How the Midwest Has Shaped a Unique Vegetarian Diet

The vegetarian movement in the Midwest is a modern, meat-free version of the comfort food that many of us grew up on. Think sunny backyard barbecues with tables filled to the brim with macaroni and cheese, corn succotash, deviled eggs, big bowls of grain salad, burgers, sandwiches, puddings, and cookies. And then there's the family diner's locally famous coffee, pies, biscuits and gravy, Reubens, subs, and french fries. Our vegetarian movement has meat-free versions of all these cozy classics.

Most Midwesterners don't understand why anyone would give up eating meat (as a Midwesterner, I can say this!). The coasts have their vegan juice bars and a seemingly endless array of upscale vegetarian restaurants, while many of us Midwesterners are more likely to see cattle farms and fresh dairy stands on our drive to work. But here's the truth, our vegetarian heartland culture is there, it's just simply not as easy to find as it is in other regions.

Despite the Midwestern vegetarian movement taking shape for the last decade, juice bars and raw cuisine restaurants are few and far between here in Midwest America. Our brutal winter discourages light meals for many months of the year. Instead, Midwestern vegetarian cuisine is based on the hearty fare that our forebears grew in their backyards decades ago. I like to think of our veggie food movement as nothing short of cozy, with meat-free versions of many comfort foods you'd find at a holiday table or local diner. We have the well-known meat-free Chicago Diner in the Windy City, which features comfort food from toasted ravioli to a vegan Reuben to biscuits and "sausage" gravy; the first all-vegan deli in Minneapolis, the Herbivorous Butcher, that sells vegan "meats" inspired by the meat markets nearby; and vegan chef and cookbook author Isa Chandra Moskowitz's upscale vegan restaurant in Omaha, featuring local food with a fancy twist with dishes like Mac and Shews, and Curry Cauliflower Steaks.

Although we've removed the meat from our plates, traditionally the centerpiece of any meal here, we have maintained that essential practice of eating off the land that has been the basis for Midwestern cuisine for more than 150 years. Our meals are still filled with Michigan cherries, Iowa corn, Indiana apples, Wisconsin dairy, Illinois wheat, and all the other nutritious ingredients that thrive in our soil and climate.

This book is a collection of modern Midwestern recipes. The dishes are based on the Midwest's selection of produce and many of them have been inspired by the Midwest's meat-centric tradition. I've also included dishes inspired by the pioneering vegetarian restaurants in the region. You will find veggie-stuffed pasties that coal miners in northern Michigan ate years ago and barbecue rub inspired by Kansas's legendary barbecue sauce. My takes on these traditional recipes eliminate processed ingredients and animal products, and instead rely on the bountiful produce and grains growing right down the street from us.

What you won't find here are the "church basement" recipes of our grandparents; sorry, no Jell-O molds or hot dishes topped with Tater Tots. You also won't find gimmicky regional recipes like St. Louis gooey butter cake or Cincinnati chili—although they are fun dishes to try when in the area, they're not about cooking with fresh ingredients in your kitchen.

These recipes are meant to inspire everyone, of all areas, while also exposing you to a few dishes that may be new to you. Enjoy!

spring

farmers' market day

recipes loaded with fresh produce
found at your local market

NO SPRAY

'ANNE'
GOLDEN
RASPBERRY

FALL BEARING

GOOD TASTE · LARGE FRUIT
VIGOROUS
HARDY

$10

NO SPRAY

'HERITAGE'
RED
RASPBERRY

LATE AUGUST · EARLY SEPTEMBER
EVERBEARING

HARDY · LONG LIVED · EASY

$10

When I'm in a new city, I go to the farmers' market, as they reveal so much. Is this a city built on produce because of all the rich soil in nearby gardens, or do they have a large selection of local cheeses from the area's dairy farms? Or maybe they pride themselves on handmade goods like soaps or freshly baked bread? Do they have a market that is open every day out of demand, or does it take place once a week as a social gathering? They're always different, there are always new discoveries, and there is always something new to eat and someone new to learn from, whether it be a farmer, maker, gardener, or artist.

Going to new markets when traveling is amusing, but making a habit out of going to the same market is a weekly adventure. Here in Bloomington, our biggest market is on Saturday morning, and I've developed a routine that revolves around going. I always wake up early, drink one cup of coffee in bed (hey, it's Saturday—a girl's got to indulge herself), and then take a leisurely walk to the market, passing by sleepy-eyed neighbors drinking coffee on their porches and newly blossoming flowers on the sidewalk's edge. The walk is about twenty minutes, and I love the silence of the neighborhood in the morning.

Produce also has a way of guaranteeing that no two markets are the same; every week there is something new in season with only faint hints here and there of last month's bountiful fruit or vegetable. I spend hours weaving in and out of the aisles, investigating every item I've never heard of, and stocking up on essentials for the week. Whether it's the time of year for ramps or morels or sour cherries, I always try to buy a good amount of at least one new item a week because there's no guarantee it will be there the following Saturday.

After an hour of blissful shopping, I usually stroll over to the food vendors for a focaccia roll and lavender lemonade. After fueling up on pillowy bread and a sweet beverage, I make my way home with a bagful of inspiration and a mind brimming with ideas.

Once I've arrived back home, it's time to cook up all the produce from my market trip. The only thing more satisfying to do on Saturdays than going to the market is preparing delicious masterpieces with the bounty of produce you picked up that day. No leisurely market visit is complete without an equally peaceful afternoon in your kitchen, so roll up your sleeves, and let's get cooking!

Sweet Potato, Feta & Chive Muffins

These savory muffins are perfect for the early spring when root vegetables are still abundant but spring greens, like chives, are starting to pop up. You can, of course, also substitute other herbs and cooked vegetables depending on what is in season. The feta and Parmesan give these savory bites a salty touch that complements the sweet potatoes perfectly.

These muffins make for a simple grab-and-go breakfast or a perfect side to any soup. Be careful not to overmix the dough as it will result in dense muffins.

1 Tbsp unsalted butter

2 cups [300 g] diced sweet potatoes, cut into ½-in [12-mm] pieces

½ cup [70 g] whole-wheat flour

¾ cup [105 g] all-purpose flour

1½ tsp baking powder

½ tsp salt

½ tsp smoked paprika

⅔ cup [160 ml] whole milk

1 egg, lightly beaten

3 oz [85 g] feta cheese

2 Tbsp chopped fresh chives

¼ cup [8 g] grated Parmesan cheese

Freshly ground black pepper

Preheat the oven to 375°F [190°C] and line a 12-cup muffin tin with paper liners.

In a small saucepan over medium heat, melt the butter. Add the sweet potatoes and sauté until they begin to brown, about 5 minutes. Add 2 Tbsp water, cover, and let steam until the sweet potatoes are easily pierced with a fork, about 3 minutes.

In a medium bowl, whisk together both flours, the baking powder, salt, and paprika. Make a well in the center of the dry ingredients and pour the milk and egg into the center. Whisk together the liquid ingredients, then slowly whisk in the dry ingredients until the dough just comes together (be careful not to over-mix). Using a spatula, fold in the sweet potatoes, feta, and chives.

Fill each muffin liner three-fourths full and sprinkle with the Parmesan and a pinch of pepper.

Bake until a toothpick inserted into the center of a muffin comes out clean, about 25 minutes. Serve warm or store in an airtight container in the refrigerator for up to 3 days.

Iced Rhubarb-Hibiscus Tea

This is a simple and subtle spring tea and an excellent use of fresh rhubarb. I first discovered this tea when browsing Martha Stewart's website but soon found out that it's a classic with gardeners who end up with extra produce from their rhubarb crops. This recipe is super-easy to scale up (just make sure you keep the water-to-rhubarb ratio the same) and results in a beautiful pink hue. A fruity replacement for your standard iced tea, this drink is perfect served on a sun-drenched spring day. You can even throw a little gin into it if you're feeling extra feisty.

3 large rhubarb stalks, chopped
3 cups [720 ml] water
Peel from ¼ lemon
1 Tbsp dried hibiscus
2 Tbsp honey
Ice cubes for serving
Fresh mint leaves for garnish

In a medium saucepan over medium-high heat, combine the rhubarb, water, and lemon peel and bring to a boil. Turn the heat to medium-low, cover, and simmer for 45 minutes. Add the dried hibiscus and let simmer for 15 minutes more. Remove from the heat and stir in the honey. Strain the liquid into a heatproof, airtight container, discarding the hibiscus and lemon peel. Refrigerate until chilled, at least 30 minutes or up to 3 hours. Serve chilled, poured over ice and garnished with mint leaves.

Baked Ricotta & Tomatoes with Thyme Butter

This is one of those recipes where you should just plan on eating the whole thing and not bother with making any other starters. This dip is simple and addictive and best served warm, with crackers, toast, or veggies. I recommend using an organic lemon for the zest since you'll be using the outside of the fruit, which is exposed to pesticides.

1 lb [455 g] whole-milk ricotta

1 tsp honey

1 egg

1 garlic clove, minced

1 tsp fresh thyme leaves, plus 1 tsp chopped

Fine sea salt and freshly ground black pepper

5 oz [140 g] cherry tomatoes, halved

1 Tbsp unsalted butter

Preheat the oven to 400°F [200°C]. Grease a 9-in [23-cm] round baking pan or pie pan.

In a medium bowl, whisk together the ricotta, honey, egg, garlic, 1 tsp thyme leaves, ½ tsp salt, and ½ tsp pepper.

Spread the ricotta mixture evenly into the prepared pan and gently press the cherry tomatoes, cut sides down, into the mixture.

Bake for 30 minutes and then place the butter directly on top of the ricotta and let it melt for 30 seconds. Once melted, tilt the pan to coat the ricotta with the melted butter and continue baking for 10 minutes more.

Remove from the oven and sprinkle with the chopped thyme and a little more pepper. Serve warm.

Green Salad with Savory Granola & Avocado-Lime Dressing

For me, a great salad is all about the texture. Of course, I always use the freshest produce possible, since the vegetables are not going to be cooked, but having a variety of textures guarantees that I won't get bored after a bite or two. In this salad, I use savory granola for crunch, fresh romaine for crispness, and an array of green vegetables for both flavor and structure.

DRESSING

½ ripe avocado

¼ cup [60 g] plain yogurt

1 Tbsp fresh lime juice

2 Tbsp chopped fresh cilantro

1 garlic clove

Fine sea salt and freshly ground black pepper

SALAD

2 cups [30 g] loosely packed chopped romaine or chopped kale, or a combination

½ ripe avocado, sliced

1 Tbsp fresh lime juice

2 green tomatoes, sliced

1 cup [100 g] Savory Granola (page 265)

Leaves from 2 or 3 cilantro sprigs

To make the dressing: In a high-speed blender or food processor, combine the avocado, yogurt, lime juice, cilantro, and garlic and blend until creamy. Season with salt and pepper. Store in an airtight container in the refrigerator for up to 3 days.

To make the salad: Lay a bed of romaine on a serving plate. Sprinkle the sliced avocado with the lime juice and layer on top of the romaine. Top with the green tomatoes, granola, and cilantro leaves. Drizzle with the dressing just before serving.

Tuscan Spring Vegetable Soup with Parmesan Bread

This is a spring riff on a simple Tuscan bread-and-vegetable stew called ribollita. Usually the bread is thrown into the soup, but I love giving it the French onion soup experience by topping it with bread and melted cheese at the very end. You can be flexible with what vegetables you swap in and out of the soup depending on what is in season. I tossed asparagus into this version since it's a spring favorite.

2 Tbsp olive oil

1 medium yellow onion, diced

1 medium carrot, diced

1 medium green bell pepper, seeded, deribbed, and diced

1 large celery stalk, diced

½ bunch asparagus, cut crosswise into quarters

2 garlic cloves, minced

6 cups [1.4 L] vegetable stock (page 254)

One 15-oz [425-g] can cannellini beans, drained, or 1½ cups [240 g] cooked beans (page 264)

4 Roma tomatoes, diced

3 sprigs thyme

1 bay leaf

1 cup [15 g] loosely packed chopped kale

Fine sea salt and freshly ground black pepper

6 thick slices hearty whole-grain bread

1 beefsteak tomato, cut into 6 slices

½ cup [15 g] grated Parmesan cheese

In a large stockpot over medium heat, warm the olive oil. Add the onion, carrot, bell pepper, celery, and asparagus and sauté until softened, 7 to 9 minutes. Add the garlic and sauté until fragrant, 30 seconds more. Add the vegetable stock, beans, diced tomatoes, thyme, and the bay leaf; turn the heat to high; and bring to a boil. Once boiling, turn the heat to medium-low, cover, and simmer for 20 minutes. Add the kale during the last 30 seconds of simmering. Remove from the heat and discard the thyme and bay leaf. Season with salt and pepper.

Preheat the broiler and arrange the bread in a single layer on a baking sheet. Top each bread slice with a tomato slice and a sprinkle of Parmesan. Broil just until the cheese has melted, about 30 seconds. Sprinkle a pinch of salt and pepper on each cheesy bread.

Divide the soup among six bowls and top with a piece of cheesy bread. Serve immediately.

Slow-Roasted Pistachio-Crusted Tofu with Red Chimichurri

I'm a strong believer that if you think you don't like tofu that's probably because it wasn't prepared correctly for you. Many people find tofu to be bland or plain but really it should be viewed as a blank canvas for your culinary experimentation. Tofu has the magical ability to take on whatever flavors you are trying to evoke in your dish. With this recipe in particular, peppers in adobo sauce are the secret ingredient that gives tofu the most wonderful smoky bite and hidden heat. Mix that with the crunchy pistachio crust and you have a bold dinner that is full of flavor!

One 14-oz [397-g] package extra-firm tofu

1 cup [140 g] shelled pistachios

1 Tbsp chopped green onions

1 cup [12 g] loosely packed fresh flat-leaf parsley leaves, plus more chopped parsley for garnish

3 garlic cloves, peeled

1½ Tbsp olive oil

1 medium red onion, cut into large wedges

1 pint [320 g] cherry tomatoes, halved

Fine sea salt and freshly ground black pepper

CHIMICHURRI

1 red bell pepper, seeded, deribbed, and diced

2 chipotle chiles in adobo (or more if you like it really spicy)

3 garlic cloves, peeled

½ cup [6 g] loosely packed fresh flat-leaf parsley, chopped

1 Tbsp dried oregano

1 Tbsp smoked paprika

¼ cup [60 ml] red wine vinegar

¼ cup [60 ml] olive oil

Preheat the oven to 300°F [150°C]. Oil a 9-by-13-in [23-by-33-cm] baking dish.

Wrap the tofu in a kitchen towel, place on a plate, and put a heavy pot or pan on top of the tofu (cast iron works great) for about 15 minutes. Once pressed, remove the towel and slice the tofu horizontally into 4 slabs. Place on the plate and set aside.

In a food processor, combine the pistachios, green onions, parsley, and garlic and pulse until the pistachios are the size of coarse bread crumbs. Using a pastry brush, brush ½ Tbsp of the olive oil onto the tofu and press the crushed pistachio mixture over the top of each piece. Place the tofu in the prepared baking dish in a single layer.

In a large bowl, toss the onion wedges and tomatoes with the remaining 1 Tbsp olive oil and season with salt and pepper. Pour the tomato-onion mixture around the tofu.

Bake until the pistachio crust starts to brown and tomatoes are just starting to burst, about 40 minutes.

Continued

To make the chimichurri: Meanwhile, in a food processor, combine the bell pepper, chiles, garlic, parsley, oregano, and paprika and pulse until finely chopped. With the processor running, slowly pour in the vinegar and olive oil and process until it's the consistency of a thick paste.

Place the crusted tofu on a serving plate, scoop the chimichurri over the crusted tofu, and season with salt and pepper. Serve immediately.

Savory Vegetable Cobbler with Herb Drop Biscuits

This was one of the first dishes I ever made as a vegetarian, and I remember being so impressed that something so delicious could come out of mixing together a few vegetables. Although this recipe has evolved tremendously since that first version, the basics remain the same: fresh vegetables roasted under a savory crumble. You can, of course, swap in whatever vegetables you have on hand (just try to chop them all the same size for even baking). The same goes for the topping, as any fresh herb and most cheeses will do.

Note: To make vegan, use nut milk in place of dairy milk, swap in ¼ cup [15 g] nutritional yeast for the cheddar, and use oil or dairy-free butter (such as Earth Balance) in the crumble.

1 Tbsp olive oil

1 medium sweet onion, diced

1 medium green bell pepper, seeded, deribbed, and diced

1 medium zucchini, diced

1 cup [90 g] chopped broccoli

3 garlic cloves, minced

½ tsp salt

½ tsp freshly ground black pepper

10 oz [280 g] cherry tomatoes

2 Tbsp all-purpose flour

¼ cup [60 ml] water

DROP BISCUITS

1½ cups [210 g] all-purpose flour

2 tsp baking soda

½ tsp baking powder

1 tsp sugar

1 tsp salt

½ tsp freshly ground pepper

¼ cup [5 g] fresh herb leaves (such as basil, thyme, chives, rosemary, or sage), finely chopped

½ cup [40 g] shredded cheddar cheese

6 Tbsp [85 g] cold unsalted butter, cut into large chunks

½ cup [120 ml] buttermilk

Continued

Preheat the oven to 425°F [200°C].

In a sauté pan over medium heat, warm the olive oil. Add the onion, bell pepper, zucchini, broccoli, garlic, salt, pepper, and sauté until softened, about 5 minutes. Add the tomatoes and flour and cook, stirring to coat the vegetables with flour, about 30 seconds. Add the water and cook until thickened, another minute or two. Transfer the mixture to a 9-in [23-cm] square baking dish and set aside.

To make the biscuits, in a medium bowl, combine the flour, baking soda, baking powder, sugar, salt, pepper, herb leaves, and cheddar cheese. Use a pastry blender or your hands to work the butter into the flour mixture until a coarse dough forms. Slowly add the buttermilk and gently mix until the dough just comes together into a single ball.

Drop the dough, 2 Tbsp at a time, over the vegetable mixture in three rows of 3 to make a total of 9 biscuits.

Bake until the top is browned and the inside is bubbly, 20 to 25 minutes. Scoop into bowls and serve immediately.

Roasted Vegetables with Creamy Romesco & Farro

This is the simplest of simple weeknight dinners. This recipe should be treated as a guideline for whatever veggies you have on hand, whether they're left over in your fridge or you just snatched them up because they looked so good at the market. To round out your meal, you'll get your dose of protein from the cannellini beans, which are added to the romesco sauce; they give the sauce a velvety profile without transforming the sauce's flavor too much from the traditional romesco.

The romesco sauce yields 3 cups, but you'll only need 2 for this recipe. Add the remainder to your morning eggs, enjoy it as a spread with crackers, or use it as a dip for Savory Herb Quinoa Pancakes (page 63).

FARRO

½ tsp olive oil

4 garlic cloves, minced

2 cups [360 g] farro, rinsed

5 cups [1.2 L] water

2 tsp fine sea salt

ROASTED VEGETABLES

5 cups [730 g] assorted vegetables (such as yellow onion, cherry tomatoes, sweet potatoes, russet potatoes, broccoli, asparagus, carrots), cut into 1-in [2.5-cm] pieces

2 Tbsp olive oil

1 tsp smoked paprika

1 tsp chili powder

½ tsp freshly ground black pepper

1 tsp salt

½ lemon

CREAMY ROMESCO SAUCE

One 15-oz [425-g] can cannellini beans, drained

12 oz [340 g] roasted red peppers from a water-packed jar, drained

2 garlic cloves, peeled

½ cup [60 g] slivered raw almonds

⅓ cup [75 g] tomato paste

¼ cup [5 g] flat-leaf parsley leaves, chopped

2 Tbsp red wine vinegar

1 tsp smoked paprika

½ tsp red pepper flakes

½ cup [120 ml] extra-virgin olive oil

Fine sea salt and freshly ground pepper

Continued

To make the farro: In a medium saucepan over medium-low heat, warm the olive oil. Add the garlic and sauté until fragrant, about 30 seconds. Add the farro and sauté for 30 seconds, then add the water and 1 tsp of the salt. Turn the heat to high and bring to a boil. Once boiling, turn the heat to low, cover, and simmer until the farro is chewy but still slightly firm, about 30 minutes. Drain any water that hasn't been absorbed.

To make the vegetables: Preheat the oven to 375°F [190°C]. Line a baking sheet with parchment paper.

In a medium bowl, toss together the assorted vegetables, olive oil, paprika, chili powder, pepper, and salt. Transfer to the prepared baking sheet and spread into a single layer.

Roast, stirring halfway through, until all the vegetables soften and begin to brown, about 30 minutes. Remove from the oven and squeeze the lemon juice over the vegetables.

To make the romesco: In a high-speed blender or food processor, blend together the beans, roasted red peppers, garlic, almonds, tomato paste, parsley, vinegar, paprika, and pepper flakes. With the motor running, slowly pour in the olive oil and continue to blend until a smooth sauce forms, about 30 seconds. Season with salt and pepper. Store in an airtight container in the refrigerator for up to 5 days.

Scoop the farro into bowls and top with the vegetables. Pour ½ cup [50 g] romesco sauce over the top of each serving. Serve immediately.

Ricotta Spaetzle with Lemon-Pea Pesto

This recipe is the German in me coming out. I've loved spaetzle since before I can remember, and it's not just because it's one of the only traditional German foods a vegetarian can eat. Spaetzle is just as delicious as its Italian counterpart, gnocchi, but even quicker and simpler to whip up. There is no shaping of the dough involved so you can just mix the dough and plop it into the boiling water. Since spaetzle can be pretty hearty, I love how the light pesto helps even out the dish. If you don't feel like making homemade pesto, the spaetzle is also delicious with just a little bit of melted Swiss over it or even your favorite pasta sauce.

10 oz [280 g] frozen or fresh peas

1 bunch asparagus, trimmed

½ cup [15 g] grated Parmesan cheese, plus more for garnish

2 garlic cloves, peeled

Juice of ½ lemon, plus more for serving

3 Tbsp chopped pecans

Fine sea salt

¼ cup [60 ml] extra-virgin olive oil

Freshly ground black pepper

SPAETZLE

2½ cups [600 g] whole-milk ricotta

Zest of ½ lemon

3 eggs

2 cups [280 g] all-purpose or whole-wheat flour

1 tsp fine sea salt

½ tsp freshly ground black pepper

Bring a large pot of salted water to a boil over high heat and prepare a bowl with ice-cold water. Once the water is boiling, add the peas and blanch for 2 minutes. Then add the asparagus and blanch for 2 minutes more. Using a slotted spoon or a fine-mesh wire colander, transfer the vegetables to the ice water for 30 seconds, then drain. Keep the water boiling.

Transfer 1 cup [165 g] of the blanched peas, the Parmesan, garlic, lemon juice, pecans, and ¼ tsp salt to a food processor and pulse until combined. With the processor running, slowly pour in the olive oil and process until a smooth paste forms. Taste and season with salt and pepper.

Continued

To make the spaetzle: In a medium bowl, whisk together ½ cup [120 g] of the ricotta, the lemon zest, and eggs. Whisk in the flour, salt, and pepper until a thick and sticky dough forms. Working in batches, drop 1 tsp of the dough at a time into the boiling water and repeat until the surface of the water is covered in floating spaetzle. Boil for 3 minutes and then use a slotted spoon to remove the spaetzle from the water and transfer to a clean plate. Repeat with the dough until it is all cooked.

Spoon the pesto and ½ cup [120 g] ricotta onto each of four plates and top with the remaining peas, the asparagus, and spaetzle. Season with a squirt of lemon juice, salt, and pepper. Serve immediately.

picnic

foods that travel well and are perfect for when you want to take your lunch onto a boat or enjoy it on a blanket next to a waterfall

By spring, we are all tired of being cooped up for so many months, and we want to spend as much time outside as possible. Some years, it can be hard to find a day without spring showers, but taking advantage of those rare sunny afternoons full of budding trees and blossoming flowers is a must. Grab a blanket, whip up a few of these recipes, and head out to your favorite spot in nature for a leisurely afternoon of wandering and eating.

In this chapter, you'll find an array of simple make-ahead recipes that are super-portable for your spring adventures, whether a picnic, day hike, work lunch, or afternoon snack between classes. Here, also, are ideas for packing up the food to travel.

Pimm's Punch

This punch is light and refreshing, with hints of fresh cucumber and strawberries. It is easy to whip up and looks stunning with chunks of fresh produce. Pour it into little resealable jars to take with you on your picnic or toss it all into a big punch bowl if you are throwing a party.

Instead of boiling a simple syrup, this recipe has cucumbers sit overnight in sugar to bring out all of their juices (similar to when you make strawberry short-cake!), which gives the sugar time to dissolve into the juice. There's no need to strain out any cucumber that hasn't dissolved since it'll add to the overall flavor of the drink.

You can go ahead and fill the punch bowl with ice if you'd prefer to keep it simple, but I like adding ice to individual cups to avoid ending up with a watery drink.

SIMPLE SYRUP
1 large cucumber, peeled and diced
½ cup [100 g] sugar

2 large cucumbers, unpeeled and sliced
1 large orange, sliced
1 large lemon, sliced
1 lb [455 g] fresh strawberries
Leaves from 1 bunch fresh mint
One 750-ml bottle Pimm's No. 1
2 cups [480 ml] gin
4½ cups [1 L] soda water or seltzer water
Ice cubes for serving

To make the simple syrup: In a small bowl, combine the diced cucumber with the sugar. Mix until the cucumber pieces are completely coated. Cover with plastic wrap and refrigerate at least 8 hours and up to 2 days.

In a large punch bowl, combine the sliced cucumber, orange, lemon, strawberries, and half of the mint. Pour in the Pimm's, gin, soda water, and the simple syrup and stir until combined.

If serving right away, fill glasses with ice and ladle in the punch (make sure to scoop up a few cucumber and fruit slices). Garnish with the remaining mint and enjoy!

If preparing for a picnic, divide the punch among 6 resealable mason jars and store in the refrigerator for up to 12 hours. Bring the ice cubes and remaining mint, for garnish, in a separate sealed jar and add to the drinks right before serving.

Roasted Carrot & White Bean Dip

Borrowing many of the same elements from hummus, this dip is slightly sweeter thanks to the roasted carrots and is much easier to get smooth and creamy due to the tender white beans. Whip up this dip a few hours before serving so the flavors can come together while sitting in the fridge. Serve with pita chips, celery, or cherry tomatoes.

8 oz [230 g] carrots, scrubbed and trimmed

3½ Tbsp olive oil

Fine sea salt and freshly ground black pepper

One 15-oz [425-g] can white beans (such as cannellini or great northern), rinsed

1 garlic clove, peeled

1 Tbsp fresh lemon juice

Celery stalks and pita chips for serving

Preheat the oven to 375°F [190°C].

Place the carrots in a baking dish; add ½ Tbsp of the olive oil, ⅛ tsp salt, and ⅛ tsp pepper; and toss to coat. Roast until a knife can easily slice through the center of each carrot, about 20 minutes. Remove from the oven and let cool slightly.

In a food processor, combine the roasted carrots, white beans, garlic, and lemon juice and process for about 30 seconds. With the processor running, slowly pour in the remaining 3 Tbsp olive oil and process until smooth, scraping down the sides as needed, about 3 minutes. Season with salt and pepper, transfer to a resealable container, and refrigerate for at least 2 hours before serving.

Serve the dip with celery and pita chips.

Salted Maple Pecan Butter

It's hard to go back to plain ol' store-bought peanut butter after enjoying this salted maple pecan butter on your morning toast or in your oatmeal. The pecans are roasted for deep flavor and color, and the maple syrup gives the salty butter a hint of sweetness. Use this butter anywhere you would use almond or peanut butter (think fancy pecan butter and jelly sandwiches, pecan butter cookies, and the like) or eat it by the spoonful for a quick and protein-packed snack. This is also the perfect topping for the Whole-Wheat Pumpkin & Poppy Seed Crackers (page 50).

3 cups [340 g] pecan pieces

½ tsp coarse sea salt

½ tsp ground cinnamon

2 to 3 Tbsp maple syrup (depending on how sweet you like it)

Preheat the oven to 300°F [150°C].

Arrange the pecan pieces in a single layer on a baking sheet. Roast until fragrant, about 20 minutes, stirring and rotating the pan every 5 minutes to avoid burning. Transfer to a medium bowl and let cool completely.

Put the pecans in a food processor and process until a smooth butter forms, 1 to 2 minutes, scraping down the sides as needed. Add the salt, cinnamon, and maple syrup and process until combined, about 10 seconds.

Transfer the pecan butter to an airtight container and store in the refrigerator for up to 1 month.

Whole-Wheat Pumpkin & Poppy Seed Crackers

Who needs to buy crackers when making your own is as easy as whipping up a batch of sugar cookies? These seedy crackers are the perfect crunchy vehicle for all of your dips (I recommend the Roasted Carrot & White Bean Dip on page 48), nut butters (Salted Maple Pecan Butter, page 49, anyone?), and cheese slices. Whip up a batch to impress your date on your next picnic or double the recipe for a crowd. Whoever you are making these for will be impressed that you took the time to make delicious crackers from scratch!

1 cup [140 g] whole-wheat flour

½ tsp poppy seeds, plus more for sprinkling

½ tsp ground cinnamon

½ tsp fine sea salt

1 Tbsp sugar

4 Tbsp [55 g] cold unsalted butter, cut into small cubes

¼ cup [60 g] canned pumpkin purée

In a large bowl, whisk together the flour, poppy seeds, cinnamon, salt, and sugar. Use a pastry blender or fork to work the butter into the flour mixture until a coarse dough forms. Add the pumpkin purée and mix until a large dough ball forms. Shape into a log that's 6 in [15 cm] long and 1½ in [4 cm] thick and cover in plastic wrap. Refrigerate for 1 hour. If making the dough ahead of time, freeze for up to 1 month and transfer to the refrigerator the night before baking.

Preheat the oven to 350°F [180°C]. Line a baking sheet with parchment paper.

Remove the dough from the refrigerator, slice into ⅛-in [4-mm] rounds, and transfer to the prepared baking sheet, spacing them ½ in [12 mm] apart. Sprinkle the rounds with more poppy seeds. Bake until the dough starts to brown around the edges, about 15 minutes.

Transfer the crackers to a wire rack and let cool completely. Store in an airtight container at room temperature for up to 1 week.

If taking these on a picnic, transfer them using a tin lined with parchment paper or a sturdy plastic storage container with a lid to keep them from getting crushed.

Crostini with Macadamia Ricotta and Corn-Zucchini Succotash

I love whipping up this vegan cheese when I'm going to be traveling because I don't have to worry about keeping it as chilled as dairy cheese. You should still keep this refrigerated as much as possible, but it's okay if it sits out while you drive to your favorite picnic area. If possible, look for macadamia pieces instead of whole nuts, as they tend to be cheaper and need less soaking time. If nut cheese isn't your thing (that's all right!), these crostini can be enjoyed with good-quality dairy ricotta.

My local bakery sells toasted baguette slices for a discounted price since they use their day-old bread to make them. Ask your local bakery or co-op if they have a similar option to save on time.

MACADAMIA RICOTTA

1 cup [120 g] raw macadamia nut pieces, soaked for about 30 minutes

2 Tbsp nutritional yeast

2 Tbsp fresh lemon juice

3 garlic cloves

⅛ tsp fine sea salt

2 tsp white miso paste

¼ cup [60 ml] water

SUCCOTASH

½ Tbsp olive oil

2 cups [280 g] fresh or frozen corn

1½ cups [225 g] diced zucchini

1 cup [155 g] frozen edamame

3 garlic cloves, minced

½ tsp sweet paprika

Fine sea salt and freshly ground black pepper

1 baguette, thinly sliced and toasted

3 heirloom tomatoes, thinly sliced

Leaves from ½ bunch fresh basil or mint

To make the macadamia ricotta: Drain and rinse the macadamia nuts. In a high-speed blender, combine the soaked nuts, nutritional yeast, lemon juice, garlic, salt, miso paste, and water and blend until it is spreadable but not quite smooth (it should look like ricotta). Store in an airtight container in the refrigerator for up to 3 days.

To make the succotash: In a large sauté pan over medium heat, warm the olive oil. Add the corn, zucchini, edamame, and garlic and sauté until softened, 5 to 7 minutes. Add the paprika during the last 30 seconds of sautéing. Remove from the heat and let cool slightly. Season with salt and pepper.

Top each piece of toasted bread with a spoonful of macadamia ricotta, a slice of tomato, some of the succotash, and a basil leaf. Serve warm or at room temperature.

For a picnic, if possible, bring macadamia ricotta, sliced tomatoes, succotash, sliced baguette, and basil leaves in separate resealable bags or containers and assemble just before eating.

Sloppy Janes

Although this isn't the best fare if you are traveling far, it's perfect for afternoon picnics in the backyard or on the porch. Sloppy Joes have a reputation for being "camp grub," and these Sloppy Janes are the vegan version of the classic. Although we can't all go back to camp (I wish!), we can re-create the experience through food in our own kitchens. The taste of these will take you back to the first day of camp, when you had butterflies in your stomach.

SWEET PICKLES
1 24-oz [710 ml] jar dill pickle spears
2 cups [400 g] sugar
2 cinnamon sticks

FILLING
1 Tbsp olive oil
1 medium yellow onion, diced
3 medium celery stalks, diced
2 medium carrots, diced
3 garlic cloves, minced
2 tsp ground cumin
1 tsp dried oregano
2 cups [480 ml] vegetable stock (page 254) or water
½ tsp red pepper flakes
1 tsp tamari or soy sauce
One 6-oz [170-g] can tomato paste
2 tsp rice vinegar
1 tsp honey
½ cup [60 g] finely chopped walnuts
One 15-oz [425-g] can pinto beans, rinsed
One 15-oz [425-g] can kidney beans, rinsed
Fine sea salt and freshly ground black pepper

8 burger buns or 12 slider buns

To make the pickles: Drain the pickles and cut into bite-size chunks. Place pickles back into the jar, cover with water, and soak for 24 hours. Drain and place into a large jar.

In a medium bowl or pitcher, combine the sugar and 1 cup [240 ml] of water. Stir until dissolved. Pour the mixture over cut-up pickles, tuck in the cinnamon sticks, and refrigerate for at least 48 hours and up to 6 months before serving. Store, refrigerated, in an airtight container or jar.

In a 12-in [30.5-cm] skillet over medium heat, warm the olive oil. Add the onion, celery, and carrots and sauté until very soft, 7 to 10 minutes. Add the garlic and cumin and sauté for 30 seconds more. Add the oregano, vegetable stock, red pepper flakes, tamari, tomato paste, vinegar, honey, walnuts, pinto beans, and kidney beans and simmer until the sauce is thick and fragrant, 12 to 15 minutes. Season with salt and pepper.

Divide the Sloppy Jane mixture among the buns and top with 2 or 3 pickle slices. Serve immediately.

Spicy Peanut Lettuce Wraps

This peanut sauce is so freaking good that you could put it on anything and it would turn out delicious. At least once a week, my boyfriend and I usually end up eating a big bowl of roasted or steamed veggies with just the peanut sauce over them for a flavorful and healthful dinner.

For an on-the-go meal, pack the filling, peanut sauce, and leafy wrappers separately in airtight containers and then use a spoon to assemble them once you are ready to eat. The wild rice filling can be served warm or at room temperature.

PEANUT SAUCE

One 1-in [2.5-cm] piece ginger, peeled

2 garlic cloves

2 Tbsp soy sauce

1 Tbsp fresh lime juice

2 tsp honey

1 tsp rice vinegar

½ cup [130 g] creamy peanut butter

½ cup [120 ml] water, plus more as needed

⅛ tsp red pepper flakes

2 cups [360 g] wild rice, rinsed

1 Tbsp peanut or coconut oil

1 cup [100 g] julienned carrots

1 bunch asparagus, trimmed and cut into 1-in [2.5-cm] lengths

1 medium yellow onion, sliced

1 cup [155 g] frozen edamame

2 garlic cloves, minced

2 tsp tamari or soy sauce

1 tsp rice vinegar

1 Tbsp fresh lime juice

Fine sea salt

¼ cup [35 g] sesame seeds

1 head iceberg lettuce or 2 small heads radicchio, leaves separated

To make the peanut sauce: In a high-speed blender, combine the ginger, garlic, soy sauce, lime juice, honey, vinegar, peanut butter, water, and red pepper flakes. Blend until completely smooth, about 30 seconds. (Add more water, 1 Tbsp at a time, if the sauce is too thick.) Store in an airtight container in the refrigerator for up to 4 days.

In a large saucepan over high heat, bring 6 cups [1.4 L] salted water to a boil. Add the wild rice to the boiling water, turn the heat to low, cover, and simmer until the rice has softened and the kernels puff open, about 40 minutes. Drain and set aside.

In a wok or large nonstick skillet over medium-high heat, warm the peanut oil. Once the oil is hot, add the carrots, asparagus, onion, and edamame and sauté for 7 minutes, stirring often. Add the garlic, tamari, and vinegar and sauté for 1 minute more. Mix in the reserved wild rice and sauté until completely combined, about 30 seconds. Remove from the heat, stir in the lime juice, and season with salt.

Place 3 Tbsp rice filling, 2 tsp peanut sauce, and a sprinkle of sesame seeds into an iceberg leaf and roll up. Repeat with the rest of the wrap ingredients and serve immediately.

Chocolate Chunk & Pistachio Zucchini Cookies

My favorite way to hide vegetables is to toss them into a baked good with a healthy dose of spices (carrot cake is a favorite in my house). These cookies are a sneaky way to use up those zucchinis that are overflowing at the market without anyone realizing they're eating vegetables.

My boyfriend calls these "muffin top" cookies because they are so pillowy and soft.

1½ cups [210 g] whole-wheat flour
1 tsp ground cinnamon
½ tsp baking soda
¼ cup [20 g] natural cocoa powder
½ cup [110 g] unsalted butter, at room temperature
½ cup [100 g] sugar
½ tsp vanilla extract
1 egg
1½ cups [220 g] shredded zucchini
1 cup [100 g] old-fashioned rolled oats
1 cup [180 g] chocolate chips
½ cup [60 g] chopped pistachios
Flaky salt for sprinkling (optional)

Preheat the oven to 350°F [180°C]. Line a baking sheet with parchment paper.

In a small bowl, combine the flour, cinnamon, baking soda, and cocoa powder.

In the bowl of a stand mixer fitted with the paddle attachment, beat the butter and sugar on medium-low speed until combined, about 2 minutes. Beat in the vanilla and egg just to combine, followed by the zucchini. Gradually add the flour mixture, beating just until combined (be careful not to overmix). Using a rubber spatula or wooden spoon, stir in the oats, chocolate chips, and pistachios.

Drop the dough by rounded tablespoons onto the prepared baking sheet, spacing the mounds 1 in [2.5 cm] apart. Sprinkle a few flakes of salt onto each cookie (if desired).

Bake until the edges darken, 13 to 16 minutes. Let cool slightly on the baking sheet and then transfer to a wire rack to cool completely. Store in an airtight container at room temperature for up to 2 days.

No-Bake Almond Fudge Bars

Every few years, we make a trip up to Mackinac Island, and I come back dreaming of fudge for months after. The little island has no cars, and you must travel by boat to get to it. Once you arrive, there is a tiny strip with old-timey buildings and tons of fudge shops. We also spend a ton of time biking around the island, exploring the Grand Hotel's gardens, and walking along the shoreline, but my mind always wanders back to those fudge shops.

When I got back from our last trip, I decided I had to tackle my own fudge. Although this raw version is very different from the fudge you'll find on the island, it is full of nutritious ingredients to give you a healthy enough treat to be enjoyed any time of day. As with most raw desserts, these little bars are dense with flavor and ingredients, so a little piece goes a long way.

If you haven't purchased Medjool dates before, look for them in the produce aisle, dried fruit section, or bulk area of your grocery store. They are the perfect natural sweetener for raw desserts.

CRUST
½ cup [60 g] almonds
8 oz [230 g] Medjool dates, pitted
⅛ tsp fine sea salt

FILLING
2 Tbsp coconut oil, solid form
¾ cup [60 g] natural cocoa powder
½ cup [120 ml] maple syrup
1 tsp vanilla extract
8 oz [230 g] Medjool dates, pitted and soaked in water for about 30 minutes
2 cups [280 g] raw cashews, soaked in water for about 30 minutes
⅛ tsp fine sea salt
½ cup [60 g] chopped almonds

Line an 8-in [20-cm] square baking pan with parchment paper.

To make the crust: In a food processor, combine the almonds, dates, and salt and pulse until a thick paste forms and the almonds are chopped very small. Press the almond mixture into the bottom of the baking pan to create an even crust. Refrigerate while preparing the filling.

To make the filling: In the clean bowl of the food processor, combine the coconut oil, cocoa powder, maple syrup, vanilla, soaked dates, soaked cashews, and salt and process until a creamy, lump-free fudge forms.

Pour the filling over the crust and spread into an even layer. Sprinkle the chopped almonds on top and refrigerate in an airtight container for at least 1 hour or up to 1 week.

Slice into 1-in [2.5-cm] squares while cold. Serve cold or at room temperature.

If traveling with the bars, cover each piece in plastic wrap or parchment paper.

brunch potluck

or how to feed your sleepy-eyed
friends when they come knocking
at your door at 10 A.M.

I come from a family in which all the women love to host parties. My grandmother was Queen of the Themed Dinner Party, like the pajama party that didn't start until 3 A.M. and went until breakfast time and the Noah's Ark party where everyone was required to bring two live animals. And my mother, though much more humble with her gatherings, would throw a big Fourth of July cookout and fifty-person backyard barbecues along the shores of the lake I grew up on. I never attended any of Grandma's festive gatherings, but I do remember watching the fireworks at Mom's lakeshore events. Kids would swim in the lake; moms hung out, rum and Cokes in hand, and gossiped on the big deck; fathers gathered around the grill. Every-body always had a blast, and my love for parties was cemented.

I've managed to carve out my own entertaining legacy with my memorable brunch potlucks. I love them because I can make as much or as little food as I want and know that my guests will bring the foods they like to eat. Given all the special diets these days, it's so much easier to host a potluck. I usually mention in the invi-tation what I'll be serving (entrée plus a drink is my go-to prep) so that the guests know what courses they can fill in: salads, sweets, sides, appetizers, and so on.

This chapter is filled with big-batch brunch inspirations that are perfect for your next gathering. The recipes are easy to scale up or down, depending on whether you are planning to feed your whole town or just keep it simple with a friend or two. From the Burnt Honey & Herby Citrus Soda (page 64) to the easy Chorizo-Spiced Lentils (page 66), you'll be sure to entertain your guests in style, and they'll leave filled to the brim with a delicious meal.

Savory Herb Quinoa Pancakes

This recipe is great for a group because it is easy to reheat or keep warm in an oven. I also make it at least once a week for lunch because it's filling, delicious, and beyond easy. I like to dollop yogurt on top, but if you are feeling extra adventurous, cut up a handful of cherry tomatoes and a bit of cucumber for garnish. Don't be afraid to stray a bit from the recipe and mix in your favorite herbs and spices instead of the ones listed here.

Note: No quinoa on hand? No problem. Swap in any leftover cooked grains you have in your fridge. Or just leave out the quinoa for a pancake that's slightly denser but just as flavorful.

2 cups [280 g] whole-wheat, all-purpose, or spelt flour

1 tsp baking powder

½ tsp fine sea salt

¼ tsp freshly ground black pepper

2 garlic cloves, minced

1 tsp ground cumin

1 tsp sweet paprika

2 Tbsp chopped fresh herb leaves or 1 Tbsp dried herbs (such as sage, basil, thyme, rosemary, or oregano)

1 cup [120 g] cooked quinoa

1½ cups [360 ml] whole milk

¼ cup [60 ml] olive oil or melted coconut oil, plus more for cooking

Plain yogurt for serving

In a large bowl, stir together the flour, baking powder, salt, pepper, garlic, cumin, and paprika. Make a well in the center of the dry ingredients and add the herbs, quinoa, milk, and olive oil into the center. Gradually stir the liquid ingredients into the dry ingredients until a thick batter forms.

Preheat the oven to 200°F [95°C]. Warm a large skillet over medium heat. Once hot, pour in just enough olive oil to coat the pan. Working in batches, ladle ¼-cup [60-ml] scoops of batter into the pan and cook until the bottoms are browned, 2 to 3 minutes. Flip and cook the other sides until browned and cooked through, 2 to 3 minutes more. Transfer to a baking sheet and keep warm in the oven while you cook the remaining pancakes.

Divide among plates, top with yogurt, and serve warm.

Burnt Honey & Herby Citrus Soda

Not everyone is ready to down an alcoholic Bloody Mary or mimosa first thing in the morning, so this is a great drink to offer alongside traditional brunch cocktails. This soda is a twist on lemonade that uses several varieties of citrus and rich, caramelized honey to sweeten it up. I like to split the batch and add a little bit of pomegranate juice to one half, so it looks like I've worked hard to create two completely different drinks. Let's keep that little secret between us, shall we?

½ cup [170 g] honey

½ cup [120 ml] water

1 cup [15 g] loosely packed fresh herb leaves (such as mint, basil, rosemary, and thyme)

1 cup [240 ml] fresh lime juice, plus lime slices for garnish

½ cup [120 ml] fresh orange juice, plus orange slices for garnish

½ cup [120 ml] fresh lemon juice, plus lemon slices for garnish

4½ cups [1 L] seltzer water or soda water

Ice cubes for serving

Pomegranate arils for garnish

In a small saucepan over medium heat, warm the honey and let simmer for 4 minutes, whisking occasionally. Remove from the heat, whisk in the water and add the herbs. Cover and let steep for at least 15 minutes or up to 30 minutes. Pluck out the herbs by hand and set them aside for garnish.

In a large pitcher, combine the honey syrup, lime juice, orange juice, lemon juice, and seltzer water.

Fill glasses with ice, pour the soda into glasses, and garnish with citrus slices, reserved herbs, and pomegranate arils to serve.

VARIATION:

Reduce the seltzer water to 4 cups [960 ml] and add in ½ cup [120 ml] pomegranate or cranberry juice.

Chorizo-Spiced Lentils

Being a vegetarian doesn't mean you should miss out on flavor. These lentils are spiced with the same ingredients as greasy chorizo for an intense and spicy side dish. Whip up a big batch to serve as a side for friends or halve the recipe and top with a fried egg for a complete meal for two.

1 Tbsp olive oil

1 medium yellow onion, chopped

2 garlic cloves, minced

1½ cups [300 g] brown lentils

2 chipotle peppers in adobo sauce

1 tsp ground cumin

1½ tsp smoked paprika

¼ tsp ground cinnamon

4 cups [960 ml] water, plus more as needed

2 Tbsp red wine vinegar

1 tsp fine sea salt

2 tsp dried oregano

1 Tbsp tamari or soy sauce

½ Tbsp peanut oil

¼ tsp freshly ground black pepper

In a large saucepan over medium heat, warm the olive oil. Add the onion and sauté until softened, 3 to 5 minutes. Add the garlic and lentils and sauté for 30 seconds. Add the chipotle peppers, cumin, paprika, and cinnamon and sauté for 30 seconds more. Pour in the water, turn the heat to medium-high, and simmer until the lentils are soft, about 30 minutes.

Meanwhile, in a bowl, whisk together the vinegar, salt, oregano, tamari, peanut oil, and pepper until smooth. Pour into the lentils, stir to combine, and simmer about 10 minutes. Add more water, as needed, if the lentils start to look dry.

Remove from the heat, spoon into bowls, and serve immediately.

Savory BKT Two-Grain Porridge

BKT stands for "vegan bacon, kale, and tomato" (a friendly riff on a BLT). If you've never had coconut "bacon" before, then you are in for a real treat! Although it may sound weird to turn something traditionally sweet, like coconut, into a salty and smoky topping, I promise you, it's a match made in heaven.

Porridge may sound old-fashioned, but this savory update would be welcome in any modern kitchen. The farro gives it an extra bite, but you can use all brown rice if that is what you have on hand. My secret to this creamy porridge is to simmer it low and slow.

PORRIDGE

½ cup [90 g] farro

½ cup [100 g] long-grain brown rice

4 cups [960 ml] vegetable stock (page 254) or water

One 14.5-oz [411-g] can diced fire-roasted tomatoes

½ tsp fine sea salt

½ cup [120 ml] water, plus more as needed

COCONUT "BACON"

1 Tbsp liquid smoke

½ Tbsp soy sauce

1 Tbsp maple syrup

1 cup [85 g] large unsweetened coconut flakes

2 cups [30 g] loosely packed chopped kale

1 cup [160 g] diced fresh tomatoes

Fine sea salt and freshly ground black pepper

To make the porridge: In a medium saucepan, combine the farro, rice, vegetable stock, tomatoes, and salt and bring to a boil over medium-high heat. Turn the heat to medium-low and gently simmer until most of the water has been absorbed and the grains are very soft, 45 to 55 minutes. Stir occasionally to prevent the grains from sticking to the bottom. Remove from the heat and let cool slightly.

Transfer half of the porridge to a large bowl, add the water, and use an immersion blender to blend until smooth, about 30 seconds. Return the blended porridge back to the pan and stir to combine. The porridge should be creamy and glossy. If gluey or dense, stir in more water as needed.

Continued

To make the coconut "bacon": Preheat the oven to 325°F [165°C]. Line a baking sheet with parchment paper.

In a medium bowl, combine the liquid smoke, soy sauce, and maple syrup. Fold in the coconut flakes until they are completely coated. Transfer to the prepared baking sheet and spread out into a single layer. Bake, stirring the flakes every 3 to 5 minutes, until they begin to brown around the edges, about 20 minutes. Stir the flakes more frequently toward the end of the cooking time as they are prone to burning.

Spoon the porridge into bowls and top with kale, coconut "bacon," and diced tomatoes. Season with salt and pepper. Serve immediately.

Broiled Green Tomatoes & Creamy Mascarpone Grits

Learning I could make creamy grits in the oven instead of on the stove top was a game changer for me. It was all too easy to say good-bye to standing over the stove for thirty minutes stirring. Turns out you can just throw all the ingredients into a dish and let it bake while you prep another part of your meal.

I recommend stirring mascarpone into your grits as it has a subtle flavor and lends a creamy mouthfeel. However, if it's too expensive or you can't find it at your local store, cream cheese will also do the trick. This recipe is a great way to use up those first green tomatoes of the season, and they hold their shape and juices better than ripe red tomatoes.

½ cup [70 g] fine cornmeal

1 tsp fine sea salt

⅛ tsp freshly ground black pepper

3 cups [720 ml] water

8 oz [230 g] mascarpone cheese

1 Tbsp unsalted butter

2 tsp chopped fresh herb leaves (such as basil, thyme, or sage)

2 large green tomatoes, sliced

¼ cup [8 g] grated Parmesan

Preheat the oven to 425°F [220°C]. In an 8-in [20-cm] glass oven-safe dish, whisk together the cornmeal, salt, pepper, and water. Cover with aluminum foil and bake for 30 minutes, stirring halfway through.

Remove from the oven and remove the foil. Whisk in the mascarpone, butter, and herbs until everything is combined and the butter has melted. Lay the tomato slices on top of the polenta in a single layer and sprinkle with the Parmesan. Turn on the broiler and place the polenta, uncovered, back in the oven. Broil until the Parmesan browns and the polenta is bubbling, 2 to 3 minutes. Remove from the oven and let cool for about 10 minutes before serving.

Spoon into bowls and serve warm.

Coconut Curry Shakshuka

This is one of those dishes that arose from my inability to make a decision about what to cook. One evening, I had leftover pita bread and couldn't decide whether to make curry or shakshuka to go with it. I finally just made a hybrid of the two. The end result is a creamy, aromatic tomato sauce that has just a kick of heat. Top it all with poached eggs, fresh basil, and lime juice, and use the pita bread for dipping.

1 Tbsp olive oil

1 medium green bell pepper, seeded, deribbed, and diced

1 medium yellow onion, diced

2 garlic cloves, minced

2 tsp curry powder

1 tsp sweet paprika

½ tsp ground ginger

1 tsp honey

½ tsp red pepper flakes

One 28-oz [794-g] can diced tomatoes

One 13½-oz [398-ml] can full-fat coconut milk

6 eggs

Fine sea salt and freshly ground black pepper

Fresh basil leaves for garnish

6 pieces pita or naan, warmed, for serving

Lime wedges for serving

In a 12-in [30.5-cm] skillet over medium heat, warm the olive oil. Add the bell pepper and onion and sauté until softened, 5 to 7 minutes. Add the garlic and sauté for 30 seconds. Add the curry powder, paprika, and ginger and sauté for 30 seconds more. Add the honey, red pepper flakes, tomatoes, and coconut milk; stir to combine; and simmer until the sauce thickens, 20 to 25 minutes.

Crack the eggs and slide them into the sauce, distributing them around the pan. Gently push some of the tomato sauce over the eggs to keep them from drying out. Cover the pan and cook until the eggs are completely set, 5 to 7 minutes.

Season with salt and pepper and sprinkle with basil. Serve immediately with pita and lime wedges.

Ricotta-Mixed Berry Breakfast Cake with Yogurt Frosting

Who wouldn't want to eat cake for breakfast? This indulgent breakfast treat is a moist citrusy-ricotta cake that's dotted with fresh berries. The frosting on top is made of yogurt to give it even more of an "eat it first thing in the morning" vibe. This cake can be made the day before and refrigerated overnight. Remove from the refrigerator at least an hour before serving and frost and garnish it just before your guests arrive.

1 cup [140 g] all-purpose flour

½ cup [70 g] whole-wheat flour

½ tsp baking soda

¾ cup [150 g] packed brown sugar

½ tsp fine sea salt

1 cup [215 g] whole-milk ricotta

2 eggs

¼ cup [60 ml] whole milk

1 Tbsp fresh orange juice, plus 1 tsp orange zest

1 tsp vanilla extract

1 cup [145 g] mixed fresh berries, cut into 1-in [2.5-cm] pieces if larger (such as black raspberries, red raspberries, strawberries, and blueberries), plus more for garnish

FROSTING

½ cup [120 g] Greek yogurt

¼ cup [30 g] powdered sugar, plus more as needed

Preheat the oven to 350°F [180°C]. Butter a Bundt pan.

In a large bowl, whisk together both flours, the baking soda, brown sugar, and salt. Make a well in the center of the dry ingredients and add the ricotta, eggs, milk, orange juice, orange zest, and vanilla to the center. Whisk together the liquid ingredients, then slowly whisk in the dry ingredients until just combined. Using a spatula, fold in the berries (be careful not to overmix).

Pour the batter into the prepared Bundt pan and use the spatula to distribute the batter evenly throughout the pan.

Bake until a toothpick inserted into the center of the cake comes out clean, about 50 minutes. Transfer to a wire rack and let cool while you make the frosting.

To make the frosting: In a medium bowl, whisk together the yogurt and powdered sugar until a thick frosting forms. Whisk in more powdered sugar, 1 Tbsp at a time, if the frosting is too thin to easily spread.

Spread the frosting on the cake and top with more berries. Cut into slices and serve right away.

Fruit & Yogurt Granola Tarts

Use the freshest fruit you can get your hands on since it will be the star of the show. These gorgeous tarts can be whipped up in less than twenty minutes. With a variety of shapes and colors piled high onto each tart, they are worthy of center stage. If making in winter or spring, consider topping with clementine, blood oranges, pineapple pieces, banana chunks, and strawberries. For summer, try cherries, blueberries, apricots, and melon slices. In fall, add apple slices (rolled in a little lemon juice to keep them from browning), pear slices, or persimmon chunks.

The crust ends up tasting like homemade granola since it is made out of similar ingredients. I like to think of this dish as a fancy version of a breakfast parfait.

Note: Make vegan by using coconut yogurt and nondairy butter (such as Earth Balance).

½ cup [110 g] cold unsalted butter, cut into cubes

2 cups [200 g] old-fashioned rolled oats

½ cup [60 g] chopped walnuts

2 Tbsp maple syrup

1 cup [240 g] plain yogurt

2 cups [280 g] fresh fruit, cut into 1-in [2.5-cm] pieces

Preheat the oven to 400°F [200°C]. Butter four 4-in [10-cm] tart pans.

In a food processor, combine the butter, oats, walnuts, and maple syrup and pulse until a chunky dough forms. Divide the dough among the prepared tart pans and press into the bottom and sides to create an even crust.

Bake until the crust has browned, 10 to 12 minutes. Remove from the oven and let cool. The crusts can be made up to 3 days ahead of time and stored in an airtight container at room temperature.

When the tart crusts are cooled, spread ¼ cup [60 g] of the yogurt over the bottom of each tart crust and arrange ½ cup [70 g] fruit on the top. Serve immediately.

summer

road trip

prepare-ahead food that will keep you full
and energized no matter how long the drive

I have an older brother, two stepsiblings, and three cousins who lived with us during my adolescence. I'm the youngest, so some of my family memories, though fond, are a bit blurry. My brother and I split our time between our mother's and father's houses, and our cousins lived with us at our father's. Every summer, my dad and stepmom would rent a huge eight-passenger van and take all five of us children on a two-week road trip across the country. We'd stop at roadside attractions, but big national parks were always our main destinations.

At a TV-less cabin in Utah, we all made up a skit for a variety show as our evening entertainment. We attempted a hellish hike into the Grand Canyon that was so hot and dry that ten-year-old me thought the big hole in the ground was a big waste of space. (My view has since changed.) These fond memories are why I'd plan a road trip to a national park over a cruise in the tropics any day.

Nowadays, I can't imagine the overwhelming planning and attention that went into piling five children into a van and taking them across the country. The only trips I've tackled require hopping into the car with my boyfriend and boxer dog. Whether it's just two of you or a big family, this chapter is filled with recipes to keep you fueled while traveling. It has an array of quick snacks and make-ahead meals to help you avoid the drive-through on any trip. Some of the recipes can be thrown in the backseat and others may require a small cooler, so pick whichever recipes will work best for you! And don't restrict yourself to using these recipes only for road trips; these are great portable meals and snacks for any all-day activity that may take you away from your kitchen.

HOW TO ADVENTURE LIKE A VEGETARIAN

Traveling and being away from the kitchen can be both exciting and exhausting. Unfortunately for vegetarians, traveling can add another layer of hassle, especially when the only options at the airport are deli turkey sandwiches or a burger from the fast-food joint next to your terminal. This is especially true in the Midwest. Though many cities have endless vegetarian options, if you venture as little as thirty minutes beyond the city limits, you may find yourself in a small town that hasn't caught on to a meat-free lifestyle just yet. Luckily, with a little planning, you can enjoy an adventure without having to starve.

Here are my tips and tricks for keeping my energy level up and my body nourished while on the road.

Make snacks ahead of time: Why take the time to prepare a sad and, let's be honest, most likely squished PB&J for a trip when you could take just a few more minutes to prep some flavored popcorn, energy bars, or peanut noodles as quick to-go snacks? If you are road tripping and have room for even more goodies, I'd also recommend some hard-boiled eggs and chopped-up fruit (or dried fruit, if it's a long trip). If you can't help but stick with peanut butter and jelly, swap in a fancy nut butter, some super-seedy bread, and a small-batch jam for a next-level flavor punch.

Eat at fast-food places with vegetarian items: Those french fries at McDonald's seem like they would be vegetarian but they are not, and you'd be surprised at how many other fast-food joints cut corners to offer up meals for cheap. Instead, try to find fast-food establishments that clearly mark their vegetarian options (I'm thinking of places like Panera Bread and Chipotle).

Research along the way: Even better than vegetarian-friendly chains, there are often local vegetarian or vegan restaurants where you can stop for lunch. When I'm in the passenger seat, I always search on my phone for vegan and vegetarian restaurants in the city we're passing through and have found some of my favorite restaurants this way. Another great option is to look up the local farmers' market and stop there to pick up local picnic goodies (think fresh bread, local produce, cheeses, and so on). You are sitting in the car for hours anyway; why not plan out your next food stop while you let someone else take the wheel?

Don't be afraid to ask: If you don't see a vegetarian option on the menu, don't hesitate to ask the waitstaff. I have been a vegetarian for more than ten years and have never been shot down at a restaurant; they can always find a way to accommodate my diet. If they are really struggling to figure out an option for you, suggest a few simple things that you think they could whip up based on the type of restaurant (pasta at an Italian restaurant, veggie tacos at a Mexican place, and so on).

Sage Iced Tea

I always need a drink by my side while driving long distances to keep from feeling parched. This tea will give you a small caffeine boost without the crash you may get from that drive-through latte. I prefer my teas not very sweet, so feel free to add more honey if you like yours sweeter. When making this drink for a trip, make the tea the day you plan to leave and store in an airtight container in the refrigerator until your departure. Add the ice just before leaving so it doesn't get too watered down.

10 fresh sage leaves
1 Tbsp honey, plus more as needed
2 cups [480 ml] water
2 black tea bags
Ice cubes for serving

Tear the sage leaves and place in the bottom of 2 large glasses. Smash the sage leaves with a cocktail muddler and pour in the honey.

Place the water in a small pot over high heat and bring to a boil. Remove from the heat and pour the hot water into the glasses. Add the tea bags and let steep for 5 minutes. Remove the tea bags and let the tea cool to room temperature. Discard the sage leaves, fill glasses with ice, and pour in the tea. Serve immediately.

Tahini & Coconut Date Bars with Dark Chocolate Drizzle

It used to be that I would always grab a handful of store-bought protein bars before heading out on a long trip, but then I kicked that habit and whipped up a batch of homemade bars. These loaded treats are so perfect that you'll never rely on processed bars again. I like to make them the night before my trip. Just be sure to wrap them in parchment paper to keep the chocolate from rubbing off in your bag or store them in an airtight container.

10 oz [280 g] dark chocolate chips

15 Medjool dates, pitted

¾ cup [165 g] tahini

1½ cups [120 g] unsweetened shredded coconut

1 Tbsp coconut oil, solid

½ tsp fine sea salt

2 Tbsp sesame seeds

½ cup [60 g] chopped walnuts

2 Tbsp cacao nibs or chocolate chips

Line a 10-in [25-cm] loaf pan with parchment paper.

In a double boiler set over simmering water, melt 8 oz [230 g] of the chocolate chips, whisking often. Drizzle the melted chocolate into the bottom of the prepared pan. Tilt the pan and lightly tap the bottom against the counter to evenly coat the bottom with the chocolate. Freeze until hardened, about 10 minutes.

Meanwhile, in a food processor, combine the dates, tahini, coconut, coconut oil, and salt and pulse until combined. Transfer to a large bowl and fold in the sesame seeds, walnuts, and cacao nibs.

Once the chocolate has set, remove the pan from the freezer. Pour the date mixture over the chocolate and press into an even layer.

In a double boiler set over simmering water, melt remaining 2 oz [50 g] of the chocolate chips, whisking often. Drizzle over the date mixture and freeze until hardened, about 10 minutes more.

Once the chocolate has set again, remove the loaf pan from the freezer. Slice crosswise into 16 bars. Store in an airtight container in the refrigerator for up to 4 days. Serve cold or at room temperature.

Minted Baba Ghanoush

I'd recommend storing this baba ghanoush in a cooler, but it should be okay left out for a little while since it does not have any dairy in it. Make sure to get thick pita chips or celery stalks to enjoy this dip with, so it doesn't drip into your lap while you are trying to drive. Or better yet, ask the person in your passenger seat to hand you a pita chip loaded with this dip while you drive—now that's teamwork!

Similar to how you prepare hummus, baba ghanoush is even easier to get a smooth consistency out of because of how soft the roasted eggplant ends up. The mint in this dish gives it an extra-bright flavor that complements the earthy eggplant and nutty coriander just right.

3 medium eggplants

½ cup [110 g] tahini

Juice of 1 lime

3 garlic cloves, minced

1 tsp ground coriander

Fine sea salt and freshly ground black pepper

¼ cup [3 g] packed fresh mint leaves

1 Tbsp olive oil

Preheat the oven to 375°F [190°C].

Poke the eggplants all over with a fork and place, cut-side down, on a baking sheet. Roast until they are easily pierced with a fork, about 30 minutes.

Let cool for about 10 minutes. When cool enough to handle, halve the eggplants, scoop out the flesh, and place into a blender or food processor. Add the tahini, lime juice, garlic, coriander, and 1 tsp salt and blend until the baba ghanoush is smooth, about 2 minutes. Season with pepper and additional salt.

Store in an airtight container in the refrigerator for up to 2 days. Just before serving, garnish with mint and drizzle with olive oil. Serve cold or at room temperature.

Chilled Peanut Noodles

These slightly spicy noodles are the perfect portable meal since they can be served at room temperature or chilled. The peanut butter will give you a protein boost, while the noodles will keep you full for hours. This dish is best served with peanuts and cilantro, which are added just before eating, though they can be added earlier if you don't want to carry around three separate containers. If the sauce thickens up too much after sitting in the refrigerator, just add a tablespoon of water to thin it out.

8 oz [230 g] soba noodles or whole-wheat spaghetti

1 cup [100 g] snap peas

½ cup [130 g] creamy peanut butter

1 tsp toasted sesame oil

2 Tbsp rice vinegar

1 tsp grated fresh ginger

2 garlic cloves, peeled

1 tsp honey

2 tsp hot chile sauce (such as Sriracha)

2 tsp fresh lime juice

⅓ cup [80 ml] water

1 green bell pepper, seeded, deribbed, and thinly sliced

1 carrot, cut into matchsticks

1 cup [140 g] peanuts, chopped, for garnish

Fresh cilantro leaves, for garnish

Bring a large pot of salted water to a boil over high heat. Add the soba and cook until almost al dente, 7 to 10 minutes. Add the snap peas and let boil for 1 minute more. Drain the soba and snap peas and transfer to a large bowl.

In a high-speed blender, combine the peanut butter, sesame oil, rice vinegar, ginger, garlic, honey, chile sauce, lime juice, and water and blend until smooth, about 30 seconds. Pour over the soba, add the bell pepper and carrots, and toss until everything is completely coated in the peanut sauce. Transfer to an airtight container and store in the refrigerator or a small portable cooler for up to 4 hours. Just before serving, garnish with peanuts and cilantro.

Brown Sugar & Rosemary Popcorn

The first time I saw rosemary show up in a sweets recipe, I was skeptical. But after just one taste of Isa Moskowitz's vegan rosemary cookies, I was blown away by how well the sugar complemented the earthy rosemary flavor. I decided to try the combination on popcorn one evening when I noticed my rosemary plant sitting on the windowsill.

If you've never made popcorn on the stove top, you're in for a treat as it knocks microwavable popcorn out of the water. The most delicious organic Indiana-grown kernels are available at my local co-op. I suggest finding a local source if you can—the end results are well worth the effort.

2 Tbsp peanut oil

½ cup [100 g] popcorn kernels

1 tsp fine sea salt

2 Tbsp unsalted butter

2 Tbsp brown sugar

2 Tbsp chopped fresh rosemary

In a large saucepan with a lid, pour in the peanut oil, add 2 popcorn kernels, and set over medium-high heat. Once the 2 kernels have popped, add the remaining kernels and cover the pan. When the kernels start to pop, gently shake the pan back and forth over the burner until there are several seconds between pops, about 3 minutes. Remove from the heat and transfer to a serving bowl. Add the salt and toss.

In a small saucepan over medium heat, combine the butter, brown sugar, and rosemary and cook, whisking continuously, until the butter melts and the sugar dissolves, 1 to 2 minutes. Pour the butter-sugar mixture over the popcorn and toss with a wooden spoon until the popcorn is evenly coated. Serve immediately.

If taking on a trip, transfer to a resealable plastic bag until ready to eat.

Spicy Double Chocolate Chip Biscotti

On a road trip, you just don't have control over that horrible gas-station coffee, but at least you'll have these delicious breakfast biscotti. There are no healthful frills in this recipe—they're just simple buttery biscotti that will keep you in the "treat yo' self" vacation mind-set. This biscotti has two layers: one that's almost like a chocolate chip cookies and a second layer with cocoa powder and a slight kick from cayenne pepper.

2 cups [280 g] all-purpose flour

1 tsp baking powder

1 tsp fine sea salt

¼ cup [20 g] Dutch-process cocoa powder

½ tsp cayenne pepper

6 Tbsp [85 g] unsalted butter, at room temperature

1 cup [200 g] packed brown sugar

1 tsp vanilla extract

2 eggs

¾ cup [135 g] semisweet chocolate chips

Preheat the oven to 350°F [180°C]. Line a baking sheet with parchment paper.

In a large bowl, whisk together the flour, baking powder, and salt. Pour half of the flour mixture into another bowl, then whisk in the cocoa powder and cayenne.

In the bowl of a stand mixer fitted with a paddle attachment, beat the butter and brown sugar on medium-low speed until creamy, about 2 minutes. Add the vanilla followed by the eggs, one at a time, and beat until combined, about 30 seconds.

Make a well in the center of the flour mixture without the cocoa and pour half of the butter-sugar mixture into the center. Using a sturdy spatula or your hands, fold the dough until a stiff ball forms. Fold in the chocolate chips and set aside.

Add the cocoa mixture to the remaining butter-sugar mixture and mix on medium speed until a stiff ball forms, about 2 minutes. Stir in any dry ingredients that remain at the bottom of the bowl.

Continued

Have ready a piece of wax paper that is 25-in [63.5-cm] long and dust it with flour. Transfer the cocoa dough ball to the wax paper. Dust the top of the cocoa dough and top with another layer of wax paper. Using a rolling pin, roll out the dough into a 6½-by-11-in [16.5-by-28-cm] oval that's about ½ in [12 mm] thick. Transfer to the prepared baking sheet. Repeat with the other dough ball, rolling it into a 6½-by-11-in [16.5-by-28-cm] oval that's about ½ in [12 mm] thick. Place the rolled-out dough directly on top of the cocoa

dough. Gently press the two doughs into each other and shift around the layers as needed to cover the edges so that the chocolate chip layer covers the cocoa layer completely.

Bake for 30 minutes. Remove from the oven and carefully cut on the diagonal into ¾-in [2-cm] slices. Turn the biscotti pieces so the cut sides are facing up and bake until dry and dark around the edges, about 15 minutes more. Let cool completely. Store in an airtight container for up to 1 week.

Crispy Almond-Butter Buckeyes

Buckeye candy is a sweet usually made from peanut butter and chocolate with an opening in the top that resembles a buckeye tree nut. Traditional buckeyes have a super-sweet peanut butter center reminiscent of fudge that I have always found to be a bit overwhelming. In this version, the center is definitely sweet but the addition of crunchy rice cereal and almond butter balances it out. Anyone from Ohio might scoff at this recipe, since it veers so far from the traditional version, but I do believe this Indiana girl has made a buckeye that's worthy of being enjoyed in any state.

¾ cup [195 g] almond butter

½ cup [110 g] unsalted butter, at room temperature, plus 2 Tbsp

⅛ tsp vanilla extract

⅛ tsp fine sea salt

1 cup [120 g] powdered sugar

¾ cup [20 g] crispy rice cereal

10 oz [280 g] dark chocolate chips

Line a baking sheet with wax paper.

In the bowl of a stand mixer fitted with the paddle attachment, beat the almond butter, ½ cup [110 g] butter, vanilla, and salt on high speed until light and fluffy. Turn the speed to medium-low and gradually add the powdered sugar, beating just until combined. Using a rubber spatula, fold in the rice cereal until evenly coated.

Scoop up the batter by rounded tablespoons and roll into a ball between your slightly greased palms. Place the buckeyes on the prepared baking sheet. Continue to form the buckeyes with the remaining batter. Stick a toothpick halfway through the top of each ball and freeze until hardened, about 30 minutes.

In a double boiler set over simmering water, melt the chocolate chips and remaining 2 Tbsp butter, whisking often.

Using the toothpicks as a handle, dip the buckeyes into the melted chocolate, leaving a small circle of almond butter uncovered at the top. Return the buckeyes to the wax paper and freeze until set, about 30 minutes. Remove toothpicks from the buckeyes and serve on a platter. Store buckeyes at room temperature for up to 10 days or wrap tightly and store in the freezer for up to 3 months.

what to make with your bounty of fresh berries and cherries from an afternoon of picking

berry-picking adventure

Berries are just like tomatoes; it's next to impossible to find a wonderfully ripe and juicy-sweet berry out of season. If you've never had the pleasure of eating a berry just off the vine, then you need to correct that as soon as you can this summer. Picking your own apples is a popular activity, but most people don't realize that many places that offer fall picking also have berry picking in the summer.

Michigan is the summer vacation spot for many of us heartland folks, for good reason. The state is known for sandy beaches and vast lakes (someone once mentioned that you can't go anywhere in Michigan without being five miles from a lake), but it also has the most gorgeous cherry orchards. The orchards are a sight to see and one that many of us associate with warm summer afternoons spent adventuring out of the summer cabin.

Strawberry Gin-Gin Mule

Gin has always been my liquor of choice, so I was sold when I discovered that there was a drink just like the Moscow Mule but with gin instead of vodka. This cocktail is slightly sweet from the fruit but also has a spicy kick to it from the ginger beer. It's refreshing enough for the summer but warming enough for cool nights as well. Many people add simple syrup to their Gin-Gin Mules, but I find the drink to be sweet enough already, thanks to the ginger beer, so you won't find it in my version here. If strawberries aren't at their peak, swap in any ripe berry that you have on hand.

3 fresh strawberries, hulled

5 torn fresh mint leaves, plus 1 sprig for garnish

1 tsp fresh lime juice

1½ oz [45 ml] gin

4 oz [120 ml] ginger beer

2 oz [120 ml] sparkling water

Ice cubes for serving

In the bottom of a tall glass, combine the strawberries and mint leaves and smash with a cocktail muddler or the end of a wooden spoon. Add the lime juice, gin, ginger beer, sparkling water, and a handful of ice and stir with a long-handled spoon. Garnish with the mint sprig and serve immediately.

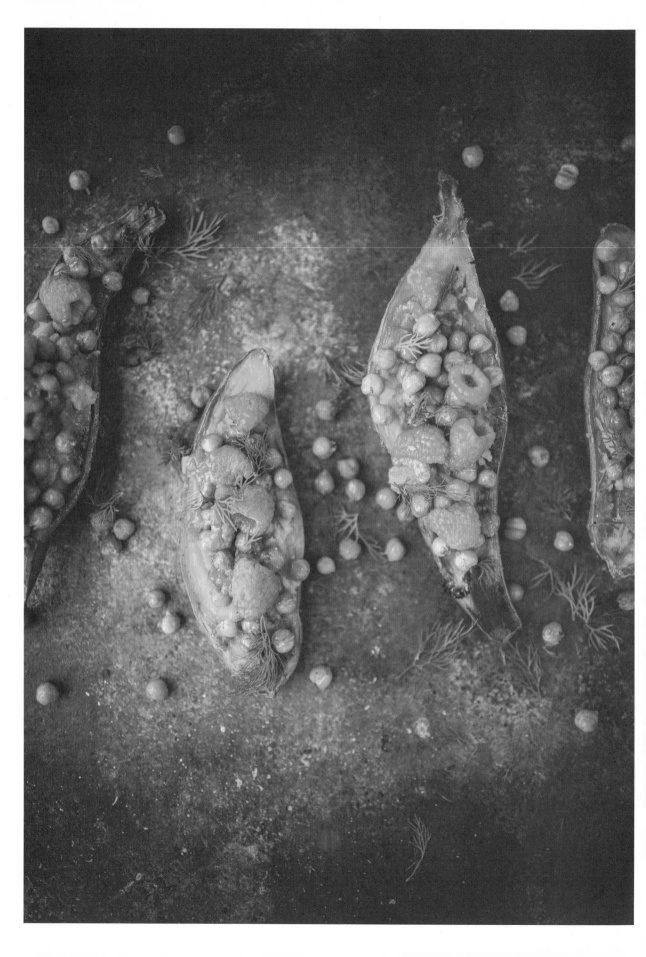

Baked Sweet Potato with Roasted Chickpeas, Raspberries & Chèvre

I had never eaten a good raspberry until I started picking them myself. At some point in my childhood, I tasted a really mushy, tart raspberry from the grocery store and decided to swear off them forever. It wasn't until I started picking my own that I discovered this delicate fruit actually bursts with flavor when ripe. A raspberry is one of the most fragile fruits out there, so make sure to buy or pick them only when they are at their peak. The variety our local farms and orchards grow aren't ready to harvest until late summer. So right when I think berry season is over, these little red jewels pop up ripe and delicious.

This recipe is a dressed-up version of the traditional baked potato; I've swapped in nutrient-dense sweet potatoes and piled them high with antioxidant-rich raspberries and creamy chèvre for the perfect combo of juicy-sweet and savory.

2 sweet potatoes, scrubbed and halved lengthwise

1 Tbsp olive oil

Fine sea salt and freshly ground black pepper

One 15-oz [425-g] can chickpeas or 1½ cups [240 g] cooked chickpeas (page 264), rinsed

½ Tbsp ground cinnamon

6 oz [170 g] fresh raspberries

2 oz [55 g] chèvre

2 Tbsp chopped fresh dill

Preheat the oven to 400°F [200°C]. Line a large baking sheet with parchment paper.

Place the sweet potatoes, cut-sides down, on the prepared baking sheet and drizzle with ½ Tbsp of the olive oil. Sprinkle with ½ tsp salt and ½ tsp pepper and place in the oven to bake.

Meanwhile, in a small bowl, toss together the remaining ½ Tbsp olive oil, the chickpeas, and cinnamon. After the sweet potatoes have roasted for 10 minutes, add the chickpeas to the baking sheet and continue to roast. About 20 minutes later, add the raspberries and continue to roast until the sweet potatoes are tender, about 10 minutes more. Remove from the oven and let cool slightly.

Mash the sweet potato flesh lightly with a fork and top with the chickpeas, raspberries, crumbles of chèvre, and dill. Serve immediately.

Blueberry & Sweet Cheese Pierogi

If you aren't familiar with pierogi, it's a pillowy dumpling that is most commonly filled with cheesy mashed potatoes, cabbage, or an assortment of fruit fillings. Where I grew up in northern Indiana, there was a huge Polish community that happily fed homemade pierogi to the entire region. There were weekly church-organized sales and a yearly Pierogi Fest in Whiting, Indiana, that we always made a trip to.

Pierogi was always one of my favorites, so my mother and I have a tradition of making our own once or twice a year. When we first started out, we would make each individual pierogi by hand but, after a few years, we invested in a pierogi press (similar to a ravioli press) so we could quickly make double or triple batches.

We always make a batch of the traditional cheddar-potato pierogi and then a batch of sweet pierogi. Many sweet versions you find in stores are stuffed with a fruit pie filling, which is too sweet for my taste buds. I've discovered that the sweetness is toned down when you add a creamy cheese into the mix, like farmer cheese or ricotta. We've tried fruit fillings in the form of strawberries, apples, and peaches, but my favorite is the blueberry version I share here.

FILLING

12 oz [340 g] fresh blueberries

2 Tbsp sugar

2 Tbsp water

13 oz [370 g] farmer cheese or whole-milk ricotta cheese

DOUGH

6 cups [840 g] all-purpose flour, plus more as needed

1 Tbsp fine sea salt

1 cup [240 ml] whole milk, plus more as needed

¾ cup [165 g] cold unsalted butter, cut into cubes

2 eggs

6 Tbsp unsalted butter

To make the filling: In a small skillet over medium heat, sauté the blueberries, sugar, and water until a thick syrup begins to form, 7 to 10 minutes. While cooking, use the back of a wooden spoon to carefully smash the softened blueberries until they're the consistency of thick jam. Remove from the heat and set aside.

To make the dough: In a food processor, combine the flour, salt, milk, cold butter, and eggs and pulse until well combined, about 30 seconds. Add more flour, a tablespoon at a time, if the dough is too sticky. Add more milk, a tablespoon at a time, if the dough is too crumbly. (You may have to make the dough in two batches, depending on the size of your food processor.)

Continued

Transfer the dough to a floured surface and divide into four equal pieces. Wrap the dough pieces in a damp kitchen towel and set aside.

To assemble with a pierogi press: Working with two pieces of dough at a time, roll the dough into two rectangles that are about ⅛ in [4 mm] thick each. Lay one rectangle dough piece over the pierogi press, fill each pierogi indentation with 1 tsp of the cheese and ½ tsp of the blueberry mixture and place the other dough rectangle directly over the top. Push a rolling pin over the dough to seal the dumplings and turn the pierogi press over so the pierogi fall out of the press, removing any excess dough. Continue with the remaining filling and dough.

To assemble by hand: Fill a small dish with water and set aside. Working with one piece of dough at a time, roll the dough into a rectangle that's about ⅛ in [4 mm] thick. Use the rim of a 4-in- [10-cm-] wide pint glass or biscuit cutter to cut out rounds. Place 1 tsp of the cheese and ½ tsp of the blueberry mixture in the center of each round and dot a little water around the edges of the circle. Fold one side of the round over the other side to form a half-moon and use a fork to press the edges to seal the pierogi. Transfer the pierogi to a floured baking sheet and set aside. Continue with the remaining filling and dough.

Bring a large pot of salted water to a boil over high heat. Working in batches, add enough pierogi to fit in a single layer and

boil until they float to the surface, 4 to 5 minutes. Remove the pierogi with a slotted spoon and set aside on a plate.

In a large nonstick skillet over medium heat, melt 1 Tbsp of the butter. Working in batches, toss in 12 pierogi or enough pierogi to fill the pan in a single layer. Cook, stirring often, until the pierogi are brown on all sides, 7 to 10 minutes. Repeat with the remaining butter and pierogi. Serve immediately.

Any pierogi that won't be eaten right away should be boiled but not yet sautéed. To store, place in an airtight container and keep in the fridge for up to 5 days, or wrap in wax paper (to avoid sticking and freezer burn), transfer to a resealable plastic bag, and keep in the freezer for up to three months.

POTATO-CHEDDAR FILLING VARIATION:

6 medium russet potatoes, peeled and cut into 1-in [2.5-cm] chunks
½ cup [40 g] shredded sharp cheddar
2 garlic cloves, minced

Bring a large pot of salted water to a boil over high heat. Add the potatoes and boil until they are easily pierced with a fork, about 10 minutes. Drain the potatoes and transfer to a large bowl. Using a potato masher or handheld electric mixer, mash the potatoes until smooth. Fold in the cheddar and garlic until combined.

Place 1½ teaspoons filling into each pierogi. Assemble and cook or store as directed above.

Raspberry Hazelnut Pancakes

Nutty and rich hazelnuts give these pancakes a wonderful flavor that complements the ripe fruit gorgeously. Perfectly ripened raspberries are hard to come by when you aren't picking them yourself, so swap in blackberries or blueberries if you like.

Hazelnut meal is not always easy to find; when you do find it, it can be expensive. I like to make my own since it adds only a minute or two to the prep time.

Be sure your pan is hot before adding the batter, or else the batter will spread out, and you'll end up with thin pancakes.

½ cup [60 g] hazelnuts

1½ cups [210 g] all-purpose flour

1 tsp baking powder

1 tsp baking soda

½ tsp fine sea salt

½ cup [100 g] granulated sugar

1 cup [240 ml] whole milk

2 eggs, lightly beaten

6 oz [170 g] fresh red or black raspberries

1 Tbsp unsalted butter, plus more for serving

Maple syrup for serving

Preheat the oven to 200°F [95°C].

In a food processor, pulse the hazelnuts until they're a fine meal, about 20 pulses. Transfer to a large bowl; add the flour, baking powder, baking soda, salt, and sugar; and whisk together. Make a well in the center of the dry ingredients and pour the milk and eggs into the center. Gently fold the liquid ingredients into the dry ingredients until a batter just comes together. Fold in the raspberries.

In a nonstick skillet over medium heat, melt the 1 tablespoon butter. Ladle ¼ cup [60 ml] of batter into the pan and cook until the bottom of the pancake is browned, about 3 minutes. Flip and cook the other side until browned and cooked through, about 3 minutes more. If your pan is big enough to fit more pancakes without overcrowding, you can cook up to 3 pancakes at once. Transfer to a baking sheet and keep warm in the oven while you cook the remaining pancakes.

Serve warm with butter and maple syrup.

Brown Butter Skillet Cornbread with Cherries, Almonds & White Balsamic

It's not uncommon for us to take a trip up to Michigan in the summer to stay at the lake house of our family friend. There are cherry orchards scattered all throughout the state, and we usually stop at one on our way home to stock up on enough cherries to last us the whole year. We freeze any we aren't able to eat right away so we can enjoy the bounty all year long.

Making this cornbread in a cast-iron skillet results in an irresistibly crispy crust and a soft, pillowy center. I like to scatter half of the almonds and cherries on top for an eye-catching presentation, which means adding them partway through the baking process. If you prefer to skip that extra step, just fold all the almonds and cherries into the batter before baking. The nutty brown butter is the perfect complement to tangy balsamic and slightly tart cherries.

Note: If you don't have buttermilk on hand (I rarely do), just combine 1 Tbsp of lemon juice and 1 cup [240 ml] of milk and let it curdle for 5 minutes. This alternative buttermilk works just fine. This method is also a great way to make vegan "buttermilk" since you can easily substitute nut milk for cow's milk.

5 Tbsp [75 g] unsalted butter

¾ cup [105 g] all-purpose flour

½ cup [70 g] whole-wheat flour

1¼ cups [175 g] fine cornmeal

2 tsp baking powder

½ tsp baking soda

¼ cup [50 g] granulated sugar

¾ tsp fine sea salt

6 Tbsp [130 g] honey

Zest of ½ lemon

1¼ cups [300 ml] buttermilk

2 eggs, lightly beaten

½ cup [60 g] chopped almonds

BALSAMIC GLAZE

1 cup [240 ml] white balsamic vinegar

¼ cup [85 g] honey

Place a rack in the upper third of the oven and preheat the oven to 400°F [200°C].

In a 9-in [23-cm] cast-iron skillet over medium heat, melt the butter. Swirl the pan often and continue to cook until the butter foams and turns a deep brown, about 5 minutes. Remove from the heat, pour the brown butter into a glass measuring cup and let cool.

Continued

In a large bowl, whisk together both flours, the cornmeal, baking powder, baking soda, sugar, and salt. Make a large well in the center of the dry ingredients and add the honey, lemon zest, buttermilk, eggs, and cooled brown butter into the center. Whisk together the liquid ingredients, then fold in the dry ingredients until the batter is combined. Fold in half of the cherries and half of the almonds. Pour the batter into the cast-iron skillet that was used for the butter.

Bake for 20 minutes and then sprinkle the remaining cherries and almonds over the top. Continue to bake until the edges have browned and a toothpick inserted into the center comes out clean, about 5 minutes more. Let cool for 10 minutes.

To make the glaze: While the cornbread is baking, in a small saucepan over medium heat, combine the vinegar and honey and bring to a simmer. Turn the heat to medium-low and simmer, whisking often, until reduced to a third, about 15 minutes.

Drizzle the balsamic reduction over the cornbread. Cut into wedges and serve warm.

Berry Brioche Cinnamon Rolls

These cinnamon rolls have that gooey cinnamon filling that everyone loves, but they also have an extra flavor punch from the roasted berries and eggy dough. These elegant pastries are perfect for serving a crowd because you can do a lot of the work beforehand. To make ahead, let the dough rise a second time in the fridge, covered, overnight. In the morning, let the rolls rise in a warm place for an hour and then bake as directed.

½ Tbsp active dry yeast

¾ cup [180 ml] warm water (100°F/35°C)

1 Tbsp granulated sugar

1 Tbsp fine sea salt

4 eggs, lightly beaten

¼ cup [85 g] honey

¾ cup [165 g] unsalted butter, melted and cooled, plus 3 Tbsp melted

4 cups [560 g] all-purpose flour

3 Tbsp ground cinnamon

1 tsp ground nutmeg

½ cup [100 g] packed brown sugar

1 cup [140 g] fresh berries, cut into 1-in [2.5-cm] pieces (such as strawberries, blackberries, or raspberries)

⅔ cup [80 g] powdered sugar

2 Tbsp whole milk

In a small bowl, stir together the yeast, warm water, and granulated sugar and let stand until foamy, about 5 minutes.

In a large bowl, combine the salt, eggs, honey, ¾ cup [165 g] melted butter, and the yeast mixture. Add the flour and stir together with a wooden spoon or spatula until a sticky dough forms. Cover with a kitchen towel and let rise in a warm spot until doubled, about 2 hours. Transfer to the refrigerator to chill for at least 1 hour.

Transfer the dough to a floured surface. Using a rolling pin, roll out the dough into a 10-by-20-in [25-by-50-cm] rectangle.

In a small bowl, combine the cinnamon, nutmeg, and brown sugar. Using a pastry brush, coat the dough with the 3 Tbsp melted butter and then evenly sprinkle the brown sugar mixture over the top. Dot the dough with the berries.

Preheat the oven to 350°F [180°C]. Grease two 9-in [23-cm] pie pans and set aside.

Continued

With the long side facing you, roll the dough into a log and pinch the seam to seal. Cut the log into 15 to 20 pieces, depending on how big you like your cinnamon rolls. Keep in mind that they will rise a decent amount during baking. Arrange the rolls, cut-side up, dividing them evenly between the pie pans. Cover the rolls with a kitchen towel and let rise a second time in a warm place for 30 minutes or let rise in the fridge overnight.

Bake the rolls until browned on top, about 30 minutes.

Meanwhile, in a medium bowl, whisk together the powdered sugar and milk until a thick glaze forms. Drizzle over the buns while still warm and serve immediately.

Chocolate-Covered Strawberry Variations

I recommend keeping this recipe in your back pocket for when you have perfectly ripe strawberries that are just too delicious to hide in a fussier recipe. Dipping strawberries in chocolate is an easy way to make a deliciously elegant dessert or snack. I've included two recipes here: a quick one with dark chocolate and a more time-consuming version with caramelized white chocolate. For the dark chocolate strawberries, the rich dark chocolate looks gorgeous dotted with tiny pieces of pink peppercorn. For the caramelized white chocolate strawberries, the roasted black sesame seeds give the strawberries an extra irresistible crunch.

DARK CHOCOLATE & PINK PEPPERCORN STRAWBERRIES

One 10-oz [283-g] package dark chocolate chips

1 lb [455 g] fresh strawberries with stems, washed and patted dry

½ tsp crushed pink peppercorns

Line a baking sheet with wax paper.

In a double boiler set over simmering water, melt the chocolate, whisking often. Using the stems as a handle, dip the strawberries into the melted chocolate. Place the dipped strawberries on the prepared baking sheet. Sprinkle with the peppercorns and refrigerate until set, about 30 minutes. Store in the refrigerator for up to 24 hours. Serve cold.

Continued

CARAMELIZED WHITE CHOCOLATE & BLACK SESAME STRAWBERRIES

1 Tbsp black sesame seeds

12-oz [340 g] white chocolate (with at least 30% cocoa butter)

1 Tbsp peanut oil

1 lb [455 g] fresh strawberries with stems, washed and patted dry

Preheat the oven to 250°F [120°C]. Line a baking sheet with wax paper.

Place the sesame seeds in a shallow bowl and set aside.

Place the white chocolate in a baking dish, drizzle with the peanut oil, and use a spatula to coat the white chocolate in the oil. Bake for 10 minutes, then remove from the oven and stir. Continue to bake, stirring every 10 minutes, until the mixture is smooth and has turned a light caramel color, about 50 minutes. There may be times when the chocolate appears chalky and turns into solid pieces, but just continue to stir, and it should melt again.

Once the chocolate is smooth and the color of light peanut butter, remove from the oven and let cool slightly.

Using the stems as a handle, dip the strawberries into the white chocolate, then roll in the sesame seeds and transfer to the prepared baking sheet. If the strawberries are moist, then you may need to spoon the chocolate over the strawberries. Continue to dip or spoon the strawberries with the remaining chocolate. Freeze until set, about 10 minutes. Once set, store in the refrigerator for up to 24 hours. Serve cold.

cookout

an array of recipes perfect for
your next backyard hangout

The East has legendary crab boils, the South has traditional round-table home-cooked meals, and Midwesterners have grill-outs, aka cook-outs. Perhaps you've been to a "grill-out" on a Manhattan rooftop or in a Texas parking lot, but we've got you beat with grilled corn picked from the field down the street and an entire pig roasting on a spit. Yup, a whole pig. You are probably wondering how a vegetarian fits into this picture, and well, we kinda don't. At least, not until we learned to take charge of the food being served at our grill-outs. If meat is the first thing that pops into your head when you're firing up the grill, then I'm about to change that!

I spent more years than I'll admit lugging store-bought veggie burgers to grill-outs in an attempt to avoid that awkward moment when the host apologizes for not having prepared anything for the token vegetarian. Despite the fact that I loved spending the day at friends' cookouts, enjoying everything from the smell of charcoal burning to the themed cocktails, it didn't take long before my stomach refused to handle another processed bean patty. I got creative with my options and, after initial concerns that it was rude of me to bring my own food, I soon realized that people were relieved that they didn't have to worry about what I would eat. I always make enough to share, and I'm always happy when others munch down on my vegetarian additions!

Plan ahead the next time you are going to a cookout, and let your host know you'll be bringing some vegetarian goodies. Whip up the patties for your homemade burgers before you leave the house, throw together a few baconless sides, and even mix up a fruity cocktail for everyone to enjoy. Not only will your taste buds and stomach thank you joyously, but so will your host for bringing some extra goodies!

TIPS FOR COOKING ON A GRILL

Here are a few tips and general guidelines to keep in mind when preparing the grilling recipes in this chapter:

Because it's impossible to control the grill so that it's always the same temperature, use the "hand test" to gauge the level of heat. Hold your hand about 4 in [10 cm] above the coals and see how long you can comfortably keep it there. For high heat, you should only be able to hold your hand over the coals for 2 or 3 seconds; for medium heat, it should be 5 or 6 seconds, and for low heat, 8 to 10 seconds. Keep in mind that the grill times in the following pages are going to vary since no grill can be controlled exactly the same way. Check the food often to avoid burning and use your best judgment for doneness.

All the recipes in this chapter involving a grill were made and tested on a charcoal grill. You are welcome to use a gas grill for these recipes as all the same instructions and rules apply for either type of grill.

Grilling is meant to be fun; it's more hands-on than many other cooking methods but that is part of the enjoyment. It is a very social form of cooking, so let friends gather around to keep you company while you tend to the food!

Whipped Goat Cheese & Pistachio Pesto Dip

This dip can be whipped up in less than ten minutes and requires no cooking time at all. The end result is light and airy, so it's perfect for a hot summer day when you'd rather be spending time by the pool than slaving away in your kitchen. Feel free to substitute any herbs you have on hand for the pesto. Serve with crackers or chopped vegetables for a more healthful scoop. Microgreens are especially lovely as garnish, but mint and basil leaves and snipped chives are pretty, too.

⅔ cup [90 g] shelled pistachios

1 cup [20 g] packed arugula leaves

3 Tbsp chopped fresh chives

10 fresh basil leaves

5 fresh mint leaves

Juice of ½ lemon

½ cup [120 ml] olive oil, plus more for drizzling

Fine sea salt and freshly ground black pepper

4 oz [115 g] fresh goat cheese

2 cups [480 ml] cold heavy cream

Microgreens for garnish (optional)

Pita chips, crackers, or sliced vegetables for serving

Place a bowl of a stand mixer, and a rimmed plate or shallow bowl in the freezer for 10 minutes to chill.

Meanwhile, in a food processor, combine the pistachios, arugula, chives, basil, mint, and lemon juice and process until combined, about 30 seconds. With the motor running, slowly pour in the olive oil and process until the pesto is smooth. Season with salt and pepper.

Remove the chilled bowl from the freezer and attach to the stand mixer. Combine the goat cheese and heavy cream in the chilled bowl and beat at medium speed just until stiff peaks form, 5 to 6 minutes.

Spread the goat cheese mixture evenly over the bottom of the chilled rimmed plate. Spoon the pesto over the goat cheese mixture, spreading it evenly. Drizzle with olive oil and sprinkle with microgreens (if using). Serve immediately with pita chips, crackers, or vegetables.

Polenta-Coated Zucchini Fries with Quick Harissa Aioli

The polenta contributes a crunchy coating to these fries, but the centers stay soft. I give you two options for cooking these: baking these will produce a crunchy chip, and grilling them will result in smoky flavor and a softer texture, not unlike grilled zucchini. Both methods are delicious and easy.

I usually cheat and make the aioli from store-bought mayonnaise. It's still delicious, and you don't have to worry about raw eggs sitting out past their prime. Harissa is a hot-pepper paste that will add spice to any dish. If you don't have it on hand or can't find it, you can substitute Sriracha sauce for a different but still delicious flavor.

AIOLI

½ cup [120 g] mayonnaise

1 garlic clove, minced

1 tsp fresh lemon juice

3 tsp harissa

1 Tbsp olive oil

ZUCCHINI FRIES

1 cup [140 g] polenta or coarse cornmeal

1 tsp fine sea salt

½ tsp freshly ground black pepper

½ tsp sweet paprika

2 eggs

2 Tbsp water

3 medium zucchini, cut into 3-by-½-in [7.5-cm-by-12-mm] sticks

To make the aioli: In a small bowl, whisk together the mayonnaise, garlic, lemon juice, and harissa. Pour in the olive oil and whisk until completely combined, about 20 seconds.

Store in an airtight container in the refrigerator for up to 3 days.

To make the zucchini fries: Preheat a charcoal or gas grill to medium heat (see page 124) or preheat the oven to 425°F [220°C]. Line a baking sheet with parchment paper.

In a shallow dish, whisk together the polenta, salt, pepper, and paprika. In another shallow dish, whisk together the eggs and water.

Working with one zucchini stick at a time, dredge it in the cornmeal and shake off the excess. Dip into the egg mixture, then coat well in the cornmeal mixture a second time. Transfer to the prepared baking sheet, spacing them 1 in [2.5 cm] apart if baking.

To grill the zucchini: Arrange the zucchini perpendicular to the lines on the grill grate, so they don't fall into the flame. Cook, flipping them every 5 minutes or so to keep them from burning, until they begin to brown, 12 to 15 minutes.

To bake the zucchini: Slide the baking sheet into the oven and bake the zucchini, flipping once, until browned, about 20 minutes.

Serve immediately with the aioli on the side for dipping.

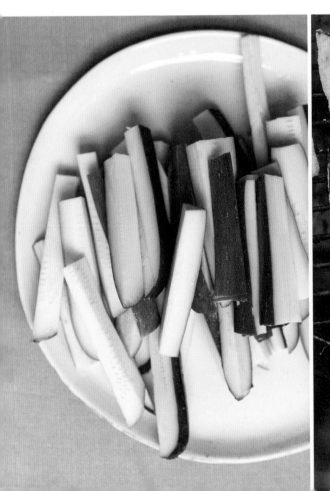

Deviled Pimiento Potato Skins

Both deviled eggs and pimiento dip are staples at community events around the heartland, so I invented this potato hybrid. If I am bringing these potato skins to an outdoor event, I will make a vegan version using vegan sour cream, vegan mayonnaise (I recommend Just Mayo), and nutritional yeast so I don't have to worry if they sit out in the sun for a while. If you don't have to worry about making it vegan, cheddar gives the filling a more pronounced pimiento dip flavor. Relish may sound like a weird addition, but I promise the tang it lends is one of the most magical parts of the delicious filling.

5 Yukon gold potatoes, unpeeled
½ Tbsp olive oil
½ tsp sea salt
Pinch of freshly ground black pepper
¼ cup [60 g] sour cream
1 Tbsp mayonnaise
1 Tbsp pickle relish
1 Tbsp pimiento peppers, sliced small
½ tsp garlic powder
½ cup [40 g] shredded cheddar cheese or ½ cup [30 g] nutritional yeast
½ tsp smoked paprika

Preheat the oven to 375°F [190°C]. Line a baking sheet with parchment paper.

Slice the potatoes in half lengthwise, place in a large bowl, and toss with the olive oil, salt, and pepper. Place the potatoes on the baking sheet, cut-side down. Bake until the potatoes are easily pierced with a fork, about 30 minutes. Remove from the oven and let cool slightly.

Scoop out the flesh of the potatoes, leaving ¼ in [6.5 mm] of flesh next to the skin, and transfer to a small bowl. Mash with a potato masher, then fold in the sour cream, mayonnaise, relish, pimientos, garlic powder, and cheddar.

Scoop the potato mixture into the potato skins, dividing it evenly. Sprinkle with paprika. Serve immediately.

Hot Honey-Glazed Peach Panzanella

Call me a carb addict, but I always find salads tastier when there is bread involved. A perfect salad is all about using fresh ingredients and having an array of textures. The sweet and spicy dressing is definitely this salad's hidden secret. This recipe is also a great way to use up any leftover or stale bread and a perfect excuse to buy an extra loaf the next time you are at the market.

One loaf French bread, sliced lengthwise

1 Tbsp olive oil, plus ¼ cup [60 ml]

10 oz [280 g] cherry tomatoes, halved

2 large peaches, halved, pitted, and sliced

¼ cup [3 g] packed fresh basil leaves, torn

1 medium cucumber, unpeeled and cut into 1-in [2.5-cm] dice

½ cup [170 g] honey

1½ Tbsp red pepper flakes

1 garlic clove, minced

1 Tbsp Dijon mustard

½ tsp fine sea salt

2 Tbsp red wine vinegar

Preheat a charcoal or gas grill to low heat (see page 124).

Brush 1 Tbsp olive oil all over the halves of bread and arrange them on the perimeter of the grill, where the heat is lowest. Cover the grill and cook, flipping often to keep the bread from burning, until browned in most spots, 2 to 5 minutes. Remove from the grill and let cool.

Tear the bread into 1-in [2.5-cm] pieces and transfer to a large bowl. Add the tomatoes, peaches, basil, and cucumber. Toss to combine.

In a double boiler set over simmering water, combine the honey and red pepper flakes. Whisk constantly until the honey reaches a temperature of 150°F [65°C], about 30 seconds. Remove from the heat and let steep for 20 minutes (longer if you like a lot of heat). Strain the honey through a fine-mesh sieve into a large bowl. Discard the red pepper flakes.

Add the garlic, mustard, salt, and vinegar to the honey and whisk together. Slowly pour in the remaining ¼ cup [60 ml] olive oil, whisking all the while, to emulsify the dressing.

Drizzle the dressing over the salad, toss to coat, and serve immediately.

Smoky Maple Baked Beans

These sweet and smoky beans come together effortlessly but do require a fair amount of cooking time, so plan ahead. Liquid smoke may be an ingredient that you are unfamiliar with, but it can be found at any major grocery store. It's become a staple in my house, because it's a great flavor booster for any recipe that would benefit from a smoky addition, which is particularly helpful when cooking vegetarian dishes. We don't all have the space (or patience) for a real smoker, and this little sauce is the perfect replacement to add extra flavor in a pinch.

2 cups [320 g] dried navy beans, soaked overnight

1 Tbsp olive oil

2 yellow onions, diced

1 green bell pepper, seeded, deribbed, and diced

2 garlic cloves, minced

¾ cup [180 ml] maple syrup

¼ cup [55 g] tomato paste

1 chipotle chile in adobo sauce, diced

1 tsp liquid smoke

2 tsp apple cider vinegar

Fine sea salt and freshly ground black pepper

In a large saucepan over high heat, combine the navy beans and 4 cups [960 ml] of water and bring to a boil. Boil, uncovered, until the beans just begun to soften, about 30 minutes. Remove from the heat, drain, and set aside.

Preheat the oven to 350°F [180°C].

In a 6-qt [5.7-L] oven-safe Dutch oven with a lid, warm the olive oil over medium heat. Add the onions and bell pepper and sauté until softened, 5 to 7 minutes. Add the garlic and sauté until fragrant, about 30 seconds more. Remove from the heat and stir in the maple syrup, tomato paste, cooked beans, chile, liquid smoke, 2 cups [480 ml] water, and vinegar. Cover and bake until the beans are very soft, about 1½ hours.

Taste and season with salt and pepper. Serve immediately.

Kansas Barbecue Tempeh Skewers

The thick glaze in this recipe is inspired by Kansas City's famous barbecue. What makes this rub Kansas City style is the molasses-tomato base, which makes for a deliciously addictive sweet and savory sauce. The tempeh and sweet potatoes are the perfect complement to the sauce, but you can also swap in any vegetables that you have on hand. You will need 10 wooden skewers soaked in water for about 30 minutes.

1 sweet potato, chopped into 1-in [2.5-cm] pieces

½ cup [160 g] molasses

¼ cup [50 g] packed brown sugar

¼ cup [60 ml] apple cider vinegar

2 Tbsp smoked paprika

2 Tbsp peanut oil

2 Tbsp tomato paste

1 Tbsp fine sea salt

½ Tbsp onion powder

2 tsp chili powder

1 tsp fresh lemon juice

½ tsp garlic powder

½ tsp cayenne pepper

One 8-oz [227-g] package organic tempeh, cut into 12 square slices

1 large yellow onion, quartered

Fill a medium pot with 1 in [2.5 cm] of water and bring to a simmer over high heat. Place the sweet potato in a steamer basket and set the basket over the simmering water. Cover and steam the potatoes until slightly softened but not mushy, about 3 minutes.

In a large bowl, whisk together the molasses, brown sugar, vinegar, paprika, peanut oil, tomato paste, salt, onion powder, chili powder, lemon juice, garlic powder, and cayenne into a thick glaze.

Pour the glaze into a resealable plastic bag, add the sweet potato, tempeh, and onion, and gently toss to coat. Refrigerate for at least 30 minutes or up to 4 hours.

Preheat a charcoal or gas grill to medium heat (see page 124).

Remove the tempeh, sweet potato, and onion from the marinade. Thread the tempeh, sweet potato, and onion onto the wooden skewers, spacing them about ½ in [12 mm] apart for even cooking.

Arrange the skewers on the grill and cook, flipping them every 3 or 4 minutes to keep them from burning, until the sweet potatoes are cooked all the way through, 12 to 15 minutes. Serve immediately.

Wild Rice Veggie Sliders with Herbed Ricotta

Can I just say, I am so glad the days of rubbery and bland veggie burgers are over and that they are finally getting the reputation they deserve as delicious and substantial! It always confuses me when I order a "veggie" burger, and there is not one vegetable in it. Don't worry; that is not what you'll find here, as there is a huge helping of chopped onion, celery, and carrots packed into these patties. These little sliders are so flavorful that they don't even need a topping (though the herbed ricotta is a delicious touch). The burgers themselves are vegan, so omit the ricotta or replace it with herbed cashew cream (page 259) if you want to keep the whole meal dairy-free.

I used Minnesota wild rice in this recipe as an ode to the wonderfully chilly state but also because of wild rice's nutty flavor and nutritional benefits (it has even more fiber than brown rice). For the binding agent, I forgo an egg for a sweet and savory paste made from dates and tahini, which complements the rice perfectly.

I prefer to make sliders since a smaller patty tends to hold its shape better, but you can also form full-size patties if you're cooking them on the stove top. To cook the burgers on the stove, heat 1 tsp of olive oil per burger in a nonstick frying pan over medium heat. Cook, covered, for 4 minutes on each side or until browned and warmed all the way through.

HERBED RICOTTA

8 oz [230 g] whole-milk ricotta

2 garlic cloves, minced

1 Tbsp chopped fresh flat-leaf parsley

1 tsp dried basil or dried oregano

½ tsp dried dill

Fine sea salt and freshly ground black pepper

VEGGIE BURGERS

⅔ cup [120 g] wild rice, rinsed

4 cups [960 ml] vegetable stock (page 254), plus ¼ cup [60 ml]

1 Tbsp olive oil

1 large yellow onion, finely diced

2 celery stalks, finely diced

3 carrots, peeled and finely diced

3 garlic cloves, minced

Leaves from 2 sprigs dill, chopped

⅓ cup [75 g] tahini

2 Medjool dates, pitted

1 tsp dried oregano

½ tsp cayenne pepper

½ Tbsp yellow mustard

⅓ cup [15 g] bread crumbs (page 256)

16 slider buns, split

Continued

To make the herbed ricotta: In a medium bowl, whisk together the ricotta, garlic, parsley, basil, and dill. Season with salt and pepper. Store in an airtight container in the refrigerator for up to 1 week.

To make the veggie burgers: In a large saucepan (with a lid) over high heat, combine the wild rice and 4 cups [960 ml] vegetable stock and bring to a boil. Turn the heat to low and simmer, covered, until tender, 40 to 45 minutes. Drain, transfer to a large bowl, and let cool slightly.

Meanwhile, in a small saucepan over medium-low heat, warm the olive oil. Add the onion, celery, and carrots and sauté until very soft, 12 to 15 minutes. Add the garlic and sauté until fragrant, about 30 seconds more. Remove from the heat and fold in the chopped dill.

In a high-speed blender or food processor, combine the tahini, dates, oregano, cayenne, mustard, and remaining ¼ cup [60 ml] vegetable stock and blend until smooth.

Add the tahini-date paste, the bread crumbs, and the sautéed vegetables to the bowl with the wild rice and fold together until combined. Transfer to an airtight container and refrigerate for at least 1 hour or up to overnight.

Using your hands, shape ¼ cup [65 g] of the mixture into a ball and then gently flatten into a patty that is about 1-in [25 mm] thick. Transfer the patties to a plate and continue to form patties with the remaining mixture. Cover and refrigerate the patties for up to 24 hours or cook them right away.

Preheat a charcoal or gas grill to medium heat (see page 124).

Arrange the patties on the grill, cover, and cook, flipping once, until warmed through, 12 to 15 minutes.

Place each patty between a bun and top with herbed ricotta. Serve immediately.

Coffee Crunch Chocolate Ice Cream with Bourbon Fudge Ripple

Summer in the Midwest is not summer without ice cream. It's always been a tradition to stop at the local ice-cream stand (or drive-up) on the way back from a sun-drenched day at the lake. It's important that you use fresh milk, cream, and eggs for this recipe since it's the base; try getting your dairy supplies from the farmers' market, where you know it'll be fresh and from humanely treated cows.

I buy my dairy products from Traders Point Creamery, which is right outside of Indianapolis, because you can visit the farm and see exactly how the animals live and are treated. After visiting the farm several times and getting up close with the cows, meeting the farmers, and walking their huge garden, I couldn't imagine wanting to support any other dairy farm.

This ice cream features chocolate-covered coffee beans and ribbons of alcoholic fudge. Enjoy it in a big waffle cone or eat it straight from the container. However you decide to eat it, this recipe is not to be missed.

1½ cups [360 ml] whole milk

1½ cups [360 ml] heavy cream

½ cup [100 g] sugar

¼ cup [20 g] Dutch-process cocoa powder

¼ tsp fine sea salt

½ cup [120 ml] strong brewed coffee, at room temperature

5 egg yolks

½ cup (85 g) chocolate-covered coffee beans, chopped

BOURBON FUDGE

⅔ cup [130 g] sugar

⅓ cup [25 g] Dutch-process cocoa powder

¼ cup [60 ml] heavy cream

4 Tbsp [55 g] unsalted butter

Pinch of salt

1 Tbsp bourbon

In a saucepan over medium heat, combine the milk, heavy cream, sugar, cocoa powder, and salt. Cook, whisking often, until the sugar dissolves, 2 to 3 minutes. Pour in the coffee and continue to cook until steaming, 5 to 7 minutes more.

Prepare an ice bath by combining ice and cold water in a medium bowl. Set aside.

In a small bowl, whisk together the egg yolks. Slowly pour ½ cup [120 ml] of the hot milk-coffee mixture into the yolks, whisking all the while, to temper them. Then slowly pour the tempered yolks into the remaining milk-coffee mixture and cook over medium heat until it's thick enough to coat the back of a spoon, 3 to 5 minutes.

Continued

Strain the mixture through a fine-mesh sieve into a glass or metal bowl. Place the bowl in the ice bath until the ice cream base cools to room temperature, about 30 minutes.

Transfer the cooled ice cream base to an airtight container and refrigerate for at least 5 hours or up to overnight.

To make the fudge: In a medium saucepan over medium-high heat, combine the sugar, cocoa powder, heavy cream, and butter and bring to a low boil. Boil for 1 minute, stirring often. Remove from the heat and stir in the salt and bourbon. Set aside and let cool completely.

In your ice-cream maker, churn the ice cream base according to the manufacturer's directions, adding in chocolate-covered coffee beans 5 minutes before the ice cream is done churning. Meanwhile, line an airtight container with parchment paper. Working in batches, pour one-fourth of the churned ice cream into the prepared container, followed by one-fourth of the fudge. Repeat with the remaining ice cream and fudge. Use a knife to swirl the fudge throughout the ice cream. Enjoy right away as soft serve or cover and freeze until easy to scoop, about 2 hours. Store in an airtight container for up to 2 weeks.

fall

fruit picking

spend a crisp afternoon picking
apples followed by an evening filled
with freshly baked treats

Maybe I'm biased because I live in Indiana, but fall is really Indiana's time to shine. Us Midwesterners dream of hitting Michigan and Minnesota in the summer for their endless lakes, but the changing leaves in the huge Hoosier National Forest is what brings tourists flocking to southern Indiana every fall.

No trip to Indiana is complete without a visit to our gorgeous apple orchards and a stop at a local diner to enjoy persimmon pudding. Southern Indiana takes their persimmons so seriously that Mitchell, Indiana, has a weeklong festival around the fruit.

This chapter is filled with recipes that showcase the fall fruit you can pick yourself: juicy apples of all varieties, firm pears, and overripe persimmons are the foraged fruits highlighted in the pages that follow.

Cranberry & Pear Turnover Breakfast Bake

I love turnovers, but I don't always have the patience to make them since it involves shaping each individual pie. I invented this simple turnover "bake" that is a delicious cross between a cobbler and a turnover with the filling on the bottom and puff pastry laid on top. It's filled with fresh fruit, oats, and maple syrup, so a bowlful of this is delicious enough for dessert but healthful enough for a breakfast treat.

8 oz [230 g] fresh cranberries

7 ripe, firm Bartlett pears, peeled and cut into 1-in [2.5-cm] dice

2 tsp fresh orange juice, plus ½ tsp orange zest

½ cup [50 g] old-fashioned rolled oats

⅓ cup [80 ml] maple syrup

2 Tbsp brown sugar

⅛ tsp fine sea salt

1 recipe Quick Puff Pastry (page 260) or 1 sheet store-bought frozen puff pastry, thawed

Yogurt or ice cream for serving (optional)

Preheat the oven to 400°F [200°C].

In a large bowl, toss together the cranberries, pears, orange juice, orange zest, oats, maple syrup, brown sugar, and salt. Pour into an 8-in [20-cm] square baking dish and bake, stirring halfway through, until cranberries are starting to burst, about 25 minutes. Carefully lay the puff pastry over the filling and trim excess dough. Cut three diagonal vent holes in the dough. Bake until puff pastry has browned, about 20 minutes more. Let cool slightly.

Serve with yogurt for breakfast or ice cream for dessert.

Ginger-Whiskey Cider

This fall cocktail is perfect to serve to friends at a scary movie night, Halloween get-together, or while hosting a backyard campfire on a chilly evening. It's full of fall spices and bourbon from our neighboring state, Kentucky. Keep the sliced fruit and spices in the pot when serving, as it makes for beautiful garnish. This recipe can be easily halved, quartered, or doubled, depending on the crowd you are expecting, just round up the measurements.

1 gl [3.8 L] apple cider

4 small lemons, sliced

2 medium apples, unpeeled and sliced

One 2-in [5-cm] piece fresh ginger, peeled and sliced

2 cinnamon sticks, plus 16 cinnamon sticks for garnish (optional)

3 cups [720 ml] whiskey or bourbon

16 whole star anise for garnish (optional)

In a large pot over medium heat, combine the cider, lemons, apples, ginger, 2 cinnamon sticks, and whiskey and bring to a simmer. Turn the heat to medium-low and gently simmer until very fragrant, 7 to 10 minutes. Turn the heat to very low to keep warm.

Pour the cider into mugs and garnish each mug with a cinnamon stick or whole star anise. Serve warm.

Spelt Crêpes Stuffed with Spiced Pumpkin, Apple & Onions

Filled with fall produce, these savory crêpes make the perfect lazy Sunday breakfast or cold-weather dinner. The sugar pie pumpkin can be swapped for butternut squash or sweet potatoes, depending on what you have in your pantry. If you don't have any spelt flour, whole-wheat flour makes a fine substitute. But I'd recommend seeking out spelt flour in your local co-op's baking aisle, if you can swing it, because it gives the crêpes an extra protein boost and a nutty flavor. Crêpes can be a bit tricky to make so don't get discouraged if your first one doesn't turn out perfectly. Keep trying and you'll quickly get the hang of it.

FILLING

1 lb [455 g] sugar pie pumpkin, peeled, seeded, and cut into ½-in [12-mm] dice

1 medium yellow onion, cut into large dice

2 apples, cored and cut into ¾-in [2-cm] dice

3 Tbsp unsalted butter

1 Tbsp chopped fresh sage

Fine sea salt

CRÊPES

1 cup [115 g] spelt flour

2 cups [480 ml] whole milk

½ tsp fine sea salt

½ tsp sweet paprika

1 tsp ground cumin

2 to 3 Tbsp unsalted butter

Plain yogurt for serving

To make the filling: Preheat the oven to 400°F [200°C]. Line a large baking sheet with parchment paper.

In a large bowl, toss together the pumpkin, onion, and apples. In a small saucepan over medium-low heat, melt the butter with the sage. Pour the melted butter and sage over the pumpkin mixture and toss to coat. Transfer to the prepared baking sheet and spread out into a single layer.

Bake, tossing halfway through, until the pumpkin is soft and onion starts to brown, about 30 minutes. Remove from the oven, season with salt, and set aside.

To make the crêpes: In a blender, combine the flour, milk, salt, paprika, and cumin and blend until completely smooth, about 20 seconds. Cover and refrigerate for about 30 minutes.

In a medium nonstick skillet over medium heat, melt just enough butter to coat the bottom of the pan. Ladle ⅓ cup [80 ml] of batter into the skillet and swirl the pan around so the batter covers the bottom completely. Cook until the crêpe sets and begins to brown, about 2 minutes. Flip and cook the other side until browned, 1 to 2 minutes more. Using a spatula, carefully remove the crêpe from pan. Stack the finished crêpes on a plate as you finish them, with paper towels or parchment paper between them. Continue cooking the crêpes with the remaining batter, adding butter to the pan after each crêpe.

To assemble the crêpes, spoon ¼ cup [45 g] of filling down the center of each crêpe and roll into a cylinder. Spoon a dollop of yogurt onto each crêpe and serve immediately.

Apple Bread Cheddar Grilled Cheese

I got the idea to use apple bread for grilled cheese from a tiny diner up in northern Michigan, where I stopped while on a road trip. We stumbled upon it by accident one morning when we needed a cup of coffee during a chilly September sunrise. I didn't end up eating the sandwich that morning, but the concept stuck with me until I got back to Indiana—I just had to try it for myself.

The sweet homemade apple bread is complemented with gooey cheese and tangy mustard for a hearty lunch or dinner. Make sure you avoid cutting your bread slices too thick or you'll have trouble getting the cheese to melt before the bread is toasted. Naturally, this is delicious served with a big bowl of tomato soup.

APPLE BREAD

2 cups [280 g] whole-wheat flour

¾ cup [150 g] packed brown sugar

1 tsp fine sea salt

2 tsp baking powder

1 tsp ground cinnamon

½ tsp ground nutmeg

1 tsp vanilla extract

1 cup [240 ml] whole milk

2 eggs

4 Tbsp [55 g] unsalted butter, melted and cooled

½ cup [125 g] applesauce

1 cup [120 g] finely diced Granny Smith apple

4 Tbsp [55 g] unsalted butter, at room temperature

9 oz [255 g] sharp cheddar cheese slices

6 Tbsp [90 g] yellow mustard

Fine sea salt and freshly ground black pepper

To make the apple bread: Preheat the oven to 350°F [180°C]. Grease a 10-inch [25-cm] loaf pan.

In a large bowl, whisk together the flour, brown sugar, salt, baking powder, cinnamon, and nutmeg. Make a well in the center of the dry ingredients and pour the vanilla, milk, eggs, melted butter, and applesauce into the center. Whisk together the liquid ingredients, then use a spatula to slowly fold in the dry ingredients until the batter just comes together (be careful not to overmix). Fold in the apple and pour the batter into the prepared pan.

Bake until a toothpick inserted into the center of the loaf comes out clean, about 50 minutes. Transfer to a wire rack and let cool completely. Cover tightly with aluminum foil and store at room temperature for up to 2 days.

Cut the loaf of bread into 12 slices. Butter each side of the bread.

In a medium skillet over medium heat, melt 1 Tbsp butter. Working in batches, lay two or three pieces of bread in the skillet and cook until the bottoms are golden brown, 2 to 3 minutes. Transfer to a plate and set aside.

Brown the bottoms of another two or three bread slices in the same manner. Flip the bread and top the browned sides with 1½ oz [40 g] of cheddar cheese, 1 Tbsp mustard, a pinch of salt, and a pinch of pepper. Place the reserved browned bread, browned side facing in, over the cheese and mustard. Cover the pan and cook until the bottom of the sandwich is golden brown, 2 to 3 minutes. Flip the sandwiches, cover, and cook until the final side is golden brown, 2 to 3 minutes more. Transfer to a serving plate and continue making the sandwiches with the remaining bread, cheese, and mustard. Serve immediately.

Fall Slaw with Maple Mustard Dressing

This slaw is the perfect side dish to all your big fall meals. Butternut squash is usually roasted, but this slaw uses raw butternut squash, showcasing its nutty flavor. Use the neck, not the bulb, as the flesh is most tender. The hardest part about this recipe is getting the carrots and butternut squash into small matchstick-like pieces; you can do this by cutting the carrots and butternut squash into ½ in [12 mm] thick matchbox slices with a sharp knife, a mandoline, or the vegetable-slicing blade in a food processor. Any of these methods will work, but the food processor is by far the fastest.

SLAW

2 medium apples, cored and thinly sliced

2 cups [220 g] thinly sliced red cabbage

1 cup [120 g] small matchstick pieces of butternut squash

1 cup [120 g] small matchstick pieces of carrot

1 Tbsp fresh lemon juice

1 Tbsp chopped fresh sage

½ cup [60 g] chopped pecans

DRESSING

2 Tbsp maple syrup

1 Tbsp Dijon mustard

1 Tbsp apple cider vinegar

½ tsp ground cinnamon

⅛ tsp fine sea salt

2 Tbsp extra-virgin olive oil

Freshly ground black pepper

1 Tbsp sesame seeds

To make the slaw: In a large bowl, toss together the apples, cabbage, butternut squash, carrots, lemon juice, sage, and pecans.

To make the dressing: In a small bowl, whisk together the maple syrup, mustard, vinegar, cinnamon, salt, and olive oil until combined. Pour over the slaw and fold until the vegetables are evenly coated. Season with salt and pepper.

Transfer to a bowl, cover with plastic wrap, and let refrigerate for at least 30 minutes before serving. Sprinkle the sesame seeds over the slaw just before serving. Serve cold.

German Fennel & Sweet Potato Pancakes

To deter you from thinking of fluffy patties made from flour and milk, you may want to call these latkes. I grew up calling these potato pancakes, as my family is all German; it was one of the few traditional German foods I could eat growing up since most are loaded with meat. There is a huge German market that pops up in downtown Chicago every December called Christkindlmarket, inspired by the outdoor markets you'd find sprinkled around Europe. Chicago in winter is painfully cold, so it's traditional for us to bundle up in our warmest attire and fend off the bone-chilling wind with at least one freshly fried potato pancake and mug of steaming mulled wine.

I'm the type of person who is always looking for ways to make a recipe healthier, but cutting back on the oil to fry the patties in this recipe will result in a soggy potato mess. (Believe me—I tried!)

2 medium sweet potatoes, peeled

1 large russet potato, peeled

1 small fennel bulb, stems removed, fronds reserved for garnish

½ cup [70 g] whole-wheat flour

2 tsp fine sea salt

2 eggs, lightly beaten

Peanut oil for frying

1 recipe Quick Spiced Applesauce (page 257) for serving

On the large holes of a box grater, grate the sweet potatoes, russet potato, and fennel into a large bowl. Wrap the grated potatoes in a kitchen towel and squeeze out the excess liquid. Transfer back to the large bowl, and add the flour and salt, and toss to coat. Fold in the eggs until the batter is fully combined.

Line a baking sheet with paper towels.

In a medium skillet over medium heat, warm ½ in [12 mm] peanut oil. Working in batches of 2 or 3, drop ¼ cup [50 g] batter into the skillet and cook until the bottom of the pancake is browned, about 3 minutes. Flip and cook the other side until browned and cooked through, about 3 minutes more. Transfer to the prepared baking sheet and cover with a kitchen towel to keep warm. Continue frying the latkes with the remaining batter, adding additional oil to the pan as needed.

Dollop the applesauce on top and serve immediately.

Deep-Dish Persimmon Pudding Pie

I was born and raised in Indiana but had never actually heard of persimmon pudding until I moved to the southern part of the state to attend Indiana University. Persimmon pudding is the local delicacy, and although the state is known for its sugar cream pie, people take persimmon pudding way more seriously around here. You can't meet a local in southern Indiana who doesn't have his or her grandma's persimmon pudding recipe handy for fall.

The filling of this pie is a cross between pudding and pumpkin pie. I decided not to venture too far from the traditional persimmon pudding recipe so as to not upset too many Indiana grandmas out there. However, I couldn't resist adding a little shortbread crust for good measure, though I kept the spices the same. It's important that you buy pulp from American persimmons (also known as Eastern persimmons), as other persimmons, such as the widely available Fuyu and Hachiya, taste completely different so the sweetness will be off.

CRUST

8 Tbsp [110 g] unsalted butter, melted and cooled

6 Tbsp [30 g] granulated sugar

2 egg yolks

2 cups [280 g] all-purpose flour

1 tsp fine sea salt

1 tsp vanilla extract

FILLING

1 pint [475 ml] American persimmon pulp

2 cups [400 g] packed brown sugar

2 eggs

2 cups [480 ml] buttermilk

2 tsp baking powder

1 tsp vanilla extract

1 tsp ground cinnamon

⅛ tsp fine sea salt

4 Tbsp [55 g] unsalted butter, melted and cooled

Whipped cream for serving

Preheat the oven to 375°F [190°C]. Grease a 9-in [23-cm] springform pan.

To make the crust: In a large bowl, using a fork or your hands, stir together the butter and sugar. Stir in the egg yolks, flour, salt, and vanilla until the dough is completely combined and a bit crumbly. Press the dough into the bottom and sides of the prepared pan.

Bake until the edges begin to brown, about 10 minutes. Remove the pan from the oven, line the edges of the crust with aluminum foil to keep it from burning, and continue baking until the center begins to gain color, about 10 minutes more. Remove from the oven and let cool completely. Lower the oven to 350°F [180°C].

Continued

To make the filling: In the bowl of a stand mixer fitted with the paddle attachment, mix the persimmon pulp and brown sugar on medium speed until combined. Add the eggs, buttermilk, baking powder, vanilla, cinnamon, salt, and melted butter and continue to mix until smooth. Pour the filling into the prepared crust.

Bake until a toothpick inserted into the center comes out clean and the top begins to brown, about 60 minutes. Let cool completely. Remove the springform, cut into wedges, and serve with whipped cream.

INDIANA PERSIMMONS

I've tried to keep the recipes in this book very accessible, so that anyone located anywhere within the United States could be able to find all the ingredients. The one exception, however, is my riff on persimmon pudding; you'll have to venture to southern Indiana to buy the pulp at a local grocery if you want to make that recipe (or order online and get some shipped to you). The type of persimmon used is known as the American persimmon (also known as the Eastern persimmon or Indiana persimmon). I've been told that it grows in regions ranging from the southern tips of Indiana, Ohio, Illinois, and Missouri down to Florida and along the East Coast, but southern Indiana's tradition of treating it like a delicacy makes it particularly available there. This is not the same persimmon as the Fuyu or Hachiya grown in California, so using those in the pudding recipe in this chapter will result in a different sweetness and end result (and is not advised).

Persimmon trees grow like crazy in southern Indiana, and they are in such abundance that people forage for the fruit for a month straight and then freeze their pulp to enjoy or sell to the local grocery stores for year-round consumption. The next time you find yourself in southern Indiana, make sure to stop at a local grocer to grab some of this delicacy or forage for some of the fruit yourself (if you are around in the fall) by collecting the ripened fruit from the ground around the trees. (Persimmons aren't ready until they fall off the tree.)

camping

food best made
over an open fire

As a kid, my family spent a lot of time camping. Most camping trips were weekend excursions to the Indiana Dunes or Lake Michigan. These spots were only fifteen-minute drives from our house but felt like worlds away in those deep woods and endless waters. On a few occasions, we went up to Minnesota for weeklong camping excursions, which required more planning. Every spring, right before camping season would start, my parents would take my brother and me to the camping store. I would immediately gravitate toward the "cooking" section, which usually consisted of freeze-dried meals. There was something about those meals that fascinated me; looking back I think it was the fact that I, as a child, was able to make biscuits and gravy or lasagna just by adding water and throwing it over the fire. I would meticulously pick out enough freeze-dried meals to last us our trip and then go off to run my meal plan by my parents, who smiled at my enthusiasm but talked me down to a meal or two. I always felt a little bummed, but I realize now that there was a reason they didn't want to eat those freeze-dried meals: they tasted awful.

Thankfully, my freeze-dried food obsession didn't last long, and I've since learned the importance of using fresh ingredients. This chapter is a mix of what we ate on the trips I took growing up and what I cook now while enjoying camping as an adult.

Note: Please read the guidelines for how to build a fire before attempting any of these recipes. Also, since no two fires are ever the same, use the cooking times provided in this chapter as suggestions but make sure you are checking your food often.

TIPS FOR COOKING OVER AN OPEN FIRE

Portion control. You won't have a refrigerator to store your leftovers, and you don't want to worry about bears or raccoons trying to get them after you've settled in the tent for the night. Make sure you cook just enough food that everyone can eat in one sitting. Luckily, most of the recipes you will find in the following chapter can be halved or doubled, so they can easily adapt to the number of people in your group.

Meal planning. Write out your menu ahead of time and plan for two hot meals a day, which will help to make sure you don't bring too much food. I find it easiest to make a fire right when I wake up for a big breakfast and then again for dinner. To avoid spending the entire day next to the campfire (unless that is your intent, which is also great!), bring easy-to-prepare snacks for the middle of the day so you don't have to worry about keeping a fire going all day long.

Make-ahead meal kits. Mix dry ingredients ahead of time. Measure out the exact amount of dry ingredients you'll need and throw them into resealable plastic bags. Not only will it save you from bringing extra food, but you also won't have to lug those measuring cups into the wild. Lastly, if you have something just labeled "biscuits" with your already-mixed flour, sugar, baking powder, and so on, then you won't have to worry about any of that prepping in the wilderness. I also like to write on the outside of the bag any special instructions. (For example, if it's pancake mix, I will write a note about how much water or milk needs to be added to it before cooking.)

Keep it cool. Bring a small cooler if planning to cook with dairy or eggs. Meat is the biggest worry if it's not kept cold, but luckily we don't have to worry about that with vegetarian recipes! To save on cooler space, I always bring the small shelf-stable containers of milk that don't have to be refrigerated (like you often see in kids' lunches).

Build a multilevel fire. It's important to spread the campfire coals around to achieve an array of cooking temperatures. Your campsite will most likely have a fire pit and a grill rack for cooking. (If not, I'd recommend investing in a cooking tripod to put over the fire.) Once the coals are very hot, spread them around, banking a larger pile on one side and a shorter pile on the opposite side. That will create a high-, medium-, and low-heat area for cooking.

CAMPSITE MEMORIES

Camping has been a favorite pastime of mine since I was a little girl. My family once took a weeklong canoeing trip in the boundary waters of Upper Michigan, but the majority of my camping experiences have been weekend car-camping adventures. Car camping does not actually involve sleeping in your car; rather, you drive up to your campsite instead of hiking in. The recipes you'll find in this chapter can be enjoyed over a fire no matter what kind of camping you choose, but they are mostly for car-camping trips since they involve a decent amount of ingredients that would be rather heavy for a backpacking trip.

Although hiking through the woods and finding streams to take dips in are definitely memorable elements of a weekend in the great outdoors, I love the calming moments at the campsite, listening to the quiet sounds of the woods, gazing into the endless forest, and making delicious food over the campfire.

1.

2.

3.

4.

5.

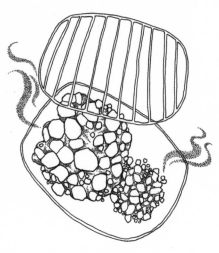

6.

A few must-have supplies for cooking over a campfire are a cutting board, can opener, knife, Dutch oven, cooking tripod (if the campsite has no grill rack), aluminum foil, tongs, wooden spoon, plates, cups, utensils, matches.

Since we can't just set the temperature for a fire the way we do for an oven, we use the same method for gauging the heat that we use for cooking over the grill: Hold your hand about 4 in [10 cm] above the coals and see how long you can comfortably keep it there. For high heat, you should be able to hold your hand over the coals for only 2 or 3 seconds; for medium heat, it should be 5 or 6 seconds; and low heat, 8 to 10 seconds.

SUPPLIES FOR BUILDING A CAMPFIRE:

» Dry leaves, newspaper, or a commercial fire starter

» Small dry twigs

» Dry wood logs purchased at the campground (Most campgrounds don't allow you to bring in your own firewood.)

» Matches or a lighter

» A bucket of water

HOW TO BUILD A CAMPFIRE

1. In the center of the fire pit at your campsite, make a small mound of dry leaves or newspaper.

2. Lean dry twigs against each other over the mounds in a teepee shape, making sure to leave a little space between the twigs for airflow so the fire doesn't suffocate and die out.

3. Use matches or a lighter to light the dry leaves or newspaper kindling. The best results are usually to light the kindling from several sides.

4. Once the twigs start to burn, add the logs, in a teepee shape, over the twigs. Make sure to leave plenty of space between the logs for airflow. Repeat this step until you have a strong fire going and continue to feed the fire with more wood as necessary.

5. Once you are ready to cook, stop feeding the fire with wood and let the flames naturally fizzle out until mostly white coals are left. Use a large stick to push the coals into a higher pile toward the back and a smaller pile toward the front to help achieve high- and low-heat areas.

6. Never leave the fire unattended. When ready to put it out, pour water over the coals, stirring the coals around with a stick to make sure they are all coated with water, until they are completely wet and no color is left in them. Be careful not to stand directly over the fire, as it will smoke while you put it out. Place the back of your hand over the coals to feel for any heat still coming off of them; if they are cold, then the fire should be completely out.

Dark Chocolate Seedy Nut Clusters

These clusters are a quick and easy make-ahead snack that will keep you fueled and satisfied when the fire isn't roaring. The chocolate shouldn't melt in the fall weather, but feel free to transport it in an airtight container to avoid a gooey mess. I threw in all of my favorite mix-ins, but you can deviate from this recipe and get creative with your favorite nuts, seeds, and dried fruit.

One 10-oz [283-g] package dark chocolate chips
½ cup [80 g] chopped dried apricots
½ cup [60 g] chopped raw almonds
¼ cup [35 g] raw pumpkin seeds
½ cup [70 g] chopped raw cashews
⅛ tsp fine sea salt

Line a baking sheet with wax or parchment paper.

In a double boiler set over simmering water, melt the chocolate, whisking often. Remove from the heat. Add the apricots, almonds, pumpkin seeds, cashews, and salt and fold together until everything is evenly coated with the chocolate.

Scoop the batter, 1 Tbsp at a time, onto the prepared baking sheet, spacing them 1 in [2.5 cm] apart. Refrigerate until the chocolate is hardened, about 30 minutes.

Store in a resealable plastic bag in the refrigerator for up to 1 week.

Smoky Sweet Potato-Egg Packets

These little pockets are beyond easy to whip up and a perfect way to make home fries and eggs all in one little packet. Swap in russet potatoes for more traditional home fries if sweet potatoes are not your thing. If not making these for breakfast, you can always skip the eggs and toss in an array of chopped vegetables and beans instead.

2 large sweet potatoes, peeled and diced

1 medium yellow onion, diced

1 tsp chopped fresh rosemary

Fine sea salt and freshly ground black pepper

4 eggs

2 Tbsp unsalted butter, cut into 4 chunks

Prepare a campfire for medium-high heat (see page 167). Put a small saucepan on the grill rack or set up a tripod over the fire. Prepare eight 12-in [30.5-cm] squares of aluminum foil.

In the saucepan, combine the sweet potatoes and just enough water to cover them. Bring to a boil and cook just until the potatoes begin to soften, about 10 minutes. Remove from the campfire and drain (in a colander, if you have it with you, or just pour out the water using a large spoon or knife to keep the potatoes from falling out). Add the onion, rosemary, ½ tsp salt, and ¼ tsp pepper and stir together until combined.

Lay out 4 of the foil squares on the picnic table. Divide the sweet potato mixture evenly among the squares, spreading the vegetables into a single layer in the center of the square. Make an egg-size well and crack an egg into it. Place a chunk of butter over each egg and sprinkle with salt. Cover with the remaining foil squares and crimp the edges up and over to seal the packets.

Place the foil packs on the grill rack or tripod and cook until the egg whites set, 5 to 12 minutes, depending on how you like your eggs. Check the foil packs often, by opening a small part of the foil packet, to keep them from burning.

Open and season with salt and pepper. Use a fork to eat right out of the foil.

Skillet Bagel Eggs with Lemon Rosemary Butter

My memories of the camping vacations of my childhood are blurry, blissful reels of luscious woods, endless lakes, and nightly campfires. Although most of the finer details have grown fuzzy with time, there is one tradition I can never forget: bagel eggs. Bagel eggs are nothing fancy—just half a bagel with an egg fried in its center. There wasn't a morning that we didn't fuel up with a bagel egg—my stepfather's campfire specialty—for breakfast. I'll never be able to enjoy them without thinking of the smoky scent of a campfire and the birds chirping in the distance. Often the memories of adventuring are as much about the food you ate as the places you visited. Adventure always makes the food taste better.

The rosemary and lemon peel infuse the butter for an extra-vibrant and flavorful breakfast. If you're making the Smoky Sweet Potato–Egg Packets and Lemony Lentil & Vegetable Soup on your camping trip, then you'll already have these two ingredients (rosemary and lemon peel) on hand.

Unless your bagels have extra-big holes in the center, you may need to cut the hole slightly larger so the egg doesn't spill over the top. To determine if my bagel hole is large enough, I usually just stick the uncracked egg in the center to make sure it fits completely.

2 Tbsp unsalted butter

2 sprigs rosemary

Peel from ½ lemon

1 bagel with a hole the size of an egg, split (see headnote)

2 eggs

Fine sea salt and freshly ground black pepper

Prepare a campfire for medium heat (see page 167). Put a cast-iron saucepan on the grill rack or set up a tripod over the fire.

In the saucepan, combine the butter, rosemary, and lemon peel and cook until the butter melts and sizzles. Add the bagel halves, cut-sides down, and crack an egg into the center of each one. Cook until the bottom starts to brown, about 3 minutes. Check the bagel often to keep it from burning. Flip and cook until the egg has completely set, 2 to 3 minutes.

Remove from the campfire, discard the rosemary and lemon peel, and season with salt and pepper. Serve immediately.

Lemony Lentil & Vegetable Soup

I recommend making this soup on the same trip that you make Mediterranean Hoagie Sandwiches (page 174), since they involve many of the same ingredients. Remember to bring only enough of each ingredient for the recipe (use resealable bags and jars to carry the measured-out portions) to guarantee that you'll have less leftover food around after the meal.

This protein-packed soup will keep you warm on chilly evenings in the dark woods and keep you full through the night. Serve with cilantro if you want to pack it along, though the bright lemon flavor is a strong enough finish on its own.

If you don't want to bring all these ingredients on your trip, prepare this soup ahead of time in your kitchen, freeze, and bring in a cooler. Just make sure you bring salt and pepper to season it just before serving.

1 Tbsp peanut oil

1 medium yellow onion, diced

3 medium carrots, diced

3 celery stalks, diced

1 medium green bell pepper, seeded, deribbed, and diced

2 garlic cloves, minced

1½ cups [300 g] dried brown lentils

6 cups [1.4 L] water

One 14½-oz [411-g] can diced tomatoes

¼ cup [60 ml] soy sauce

Juice of ½ lemon, plus lemon wedges for garnish (optional)

Fine sea salt and freshly ground black pepper

Torn fresh cilantro leaves for garnish (optional)

Prepare a campfire for medium heat (see page 167). Put a Dutch oven or large saucepan on the grill rack or set up a tripod over the fire.

In the Dutch oven, warm the peanut oil. Add the onion, carrots, celery, bell pepper, and garlic and sauté until the vegetables soften, about 10 minutes.

Add the lentils and sauté until slightly toasted, about 30 seconds. Add the water and tomatoes and simmer until the lentils have softened completely, about 25 minutes. Remove the Dutch oven from the campfire, stir in the soy sauce and lemon juice and season with salt and pepper.

Divide among six bowls, garnish with cilantro and lemon wedges (if using), and serve immediately.

Mediterranean Hoagie Sandwiches

The ingredient list for this may seem like a lot to lug, but you can mix the olive oil, vinegar, and oregano in a jar beforehand and just bring enough to put on your sandwiches. Use the provolone if you'll be car camping and have a cooler handy, but you can leave it out if you don't want to carry the cheese in your backpack all day. Finally, make sure the aluminum foil is wrapped around the sandwiches three or four times to help keep the bread from burning.

¼ cup [60 ml] extra-virgin olive oil

2 Tbsp balsamic vinegar

2 tsp dried oregano

4 hoagie rolls, split

1 medium red bell pepper, seeded, deribbed, and sliced

1 medium yellow onion, sliced

2 medium zucchinis, sliced crosswise

10 cherry tomatoes, halved

3 carrots, sliced

4 slices provolone cheese (optional)

Fine sea salt and freshly ground black pepper

Prepare a campfire for medium heat (see page 167). Prepare four 25-in [63.5-cm] lengths of aluminum foil and fold each sheet in half crosswise.

Whisk together the olive oil, balsamic vinegar, and oregano with a fork or shake together in a resealable mason jar. Set aside.

On the bottom halves of the rolls, layer the bell pepper, onion, zucchinis, tomatoes, and carrots, dividing them evenly. Transfer each roll to a piece of aluminum foil and drizzle with the olive oil mixture. Layer the provolone (if using) on top and season with a pinch of salt and a pinch of pepper. Close the hoagies with the top halves of the rolls and wrap the foil around the sandwiches three or four times.

Arrange the hoagies on the grill rack. Cook, rotating them every 2 to 3 minutes to keep the bread from burning, until the vegetables soften and the rolls are toasted, about 10 minutes. Remove the foil and serve immediately.

Caramel, Roasted Strawberries & Chocolate Cookie S'mores

There is no simpler way to wow your camping buddies then to pull out a bag of homemade graham crackers. This version veers from the traditional by avoiding the hard-to-find graham flour, using instead a heavy dose of cocoa powder. These chocolaty "crackers" (they really should be called cookies) are similar to shortbread and complement gooey marshmallows and caramel perfectly.

Prepare the cookies up to three days ahead and bring them in a resealable container so they won't get mashed or stale. Since the cookies have chocolate in them, I tuck a little caramel inside the treat for a gooey and still-sweet filling. Make sure you are sourcing gelatin-free marshmallows or these won't be vegetarian.

COOKIES

½ cup [40 g] Dutch-process cocoa powder

½ tsp ground cinnamon

2 cups [280 g] all-purpose flour

1 cup [200 g] packed brown sugar

1 tsp baking soda

½ tsp fine sea salt

8 Tbsp [110 g] cold unsalted butter, cut into small cubes

⅓ cup [115 g] honey

6 Tbsp [90 ml] whole milk

1 Tbsp vanilla extract

6 gelatin-free marshmallows

6 fresh strawberries

6 wrapped soft caramels

To make the cookies: In a food processor, combine the cocoa powder, cinnamon, flour, brown sugar, baking soda, and salt and pulse until combined. Add the butter and pulse until a coarse meal forms.

In a large bowl, whisk together the honey, milk, and vanilla. With the processor running, slowly pour in the liquid ingredients and process until a big sticky dough ball forms, 3 to 5 minutes.

Place the dough between two long sheets of wax paper and, using a rolling pin, roll the dough into a 12-in [30.5-cm] square. Transfer the wax paper and dough to a baking sheet and freeze until firm, about 20 minutes.

Line two baking sheets with parchment paper.

Remove the chilled dough from the freezer and divide into two pieces. Transfer the dough to a floured surface and roll each piece into a 12-by-16-in [30.5-by-40.5-cm] rectangle that's about ⅛ in [4 mm] thick. Cut the rectangles into 4-in [10-cm] squares and transfer to the prepared baking sheets. Freeze the dough until firm, at least 30 minutes or up to overnight.

Preheat the oven to 350°F [180°C].

Bake the cookies until firm, 20 to 25 minutes. Remove from the oven and let cool completely. Store in an airtight container for up to 3 days.

Prepare a campfire for medium heat (see page 167).

Skewer the marshmallows and strawberries onto sticks. Hold the sticks over the campfire and roast, rotating the marshmallows and strawberries often, until the marshmallows are golden brown and the strawberries soften, 2 to 4 minutes. Remove from the heat.

Lay out 6 of the cookies on the picnic table, keeping the remaining six cookies at the ready. Place one marshmallow on each of the 6 cookies, followed by one strawberry and one caramel. Top with another cookie pressing down so the marshmallow oozes to fill out the sides of the sandwich. Serve immediately by passing them out to all your friends!

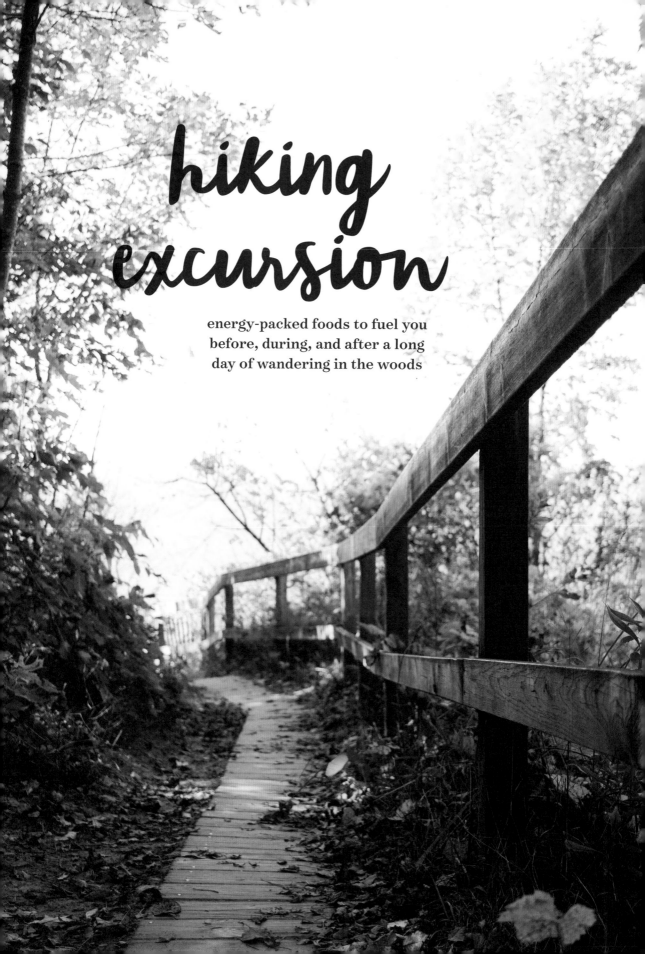

hiking excursion

energy-packed foods to fuel you
before, during, and after a long
day of wandering in the woods

I've been on one too many beautiful hikes that I stopped enjoying halfway through because my stomach started growling. You know what I'm talking about? You are walking along, taking in all the beautiful sights of nature, and your focus abruptly shifts from optimistically wanting to explore for days to immediately needing to get back to the car so you can grab that energy bar you packed. This chapter is all about foods you can throw in your pack on those hikes (whether they are full-on day trips or just a quick after-work wander through the woods) to keep you from running out of energy.

Although it's not quite as glamorous as escaping onto the trails, these snacks are also perfect for your everyday needs. Not planning a hiking excursion anytime soon? Try wrapping up the simple Peanut Butter Trail Mix Cookies (page 192) and throwing them in your purse while running errands or finishing a work assignment, or bring an already prepared Quinoa Wrap with Dill Pesto, Hazelnuts & Apricots (page 188) in your laptop bag to work when you know you won't have time to leave for lunch.

Tahini & Cocoa Breakfast Shake

The perfect breakfast for when you are in a time crunch or just looking for something sweet to fill you up before starting your day. I also love whipping this up as an afternoon snack when I am craving something chocolaty (like a brownie!) but don't want an indulgent baked good.

1 banana
¼ cup [55 g] tahini
½ cup [120 g] plain yogurt
1½ Tbsp Dutch-process cocoa powder
1½ Tbsp maple syrup
⅛ tsp ground cinnamon
½ cup crushed ice

In a blender, combine the banana, tahini, yogurt, cocoa powder, maple syrup, cinnamon, and ice and blend until smooth and creamy, about 1 minute. Transfer to a large glass and drink right away.

Sweet & Sour Michigan Pasties

There is the most amazing vegan bakery, Rainbow Bakery, about four blocks from my house. Although their specialty is doughnuts, they often make vegan versions of Midwestern classics like buckeyes and pasties that are out of this world. Although my version isn't vegan, this is my ode to my favorite baked goody at the shop. You can make these "Rainbow Bakery style" by stuffing them with pizza fillings, but I'm all about enjoying a sweet and sour center. As in so many other parts of the world, miners in the Upper Peninsula of Michigan used to eat pasties for lunch since they were filling, handheld, and easy to grab and go. These are perfect for hiking for these same reasons.

3 Tbsp olive oil

One 8-oz [227-g] package organic tempeh, cut into 1-in [2.5-cm] dice

1 medium yellow onion, cut into 1-in [2.5-cm] dice

1 green bell pepper, seeded, deribbed, and cut into 1-in [2.5-cm] dice

1 garlic clove, minced

1 large tomato, cut into 1-in [2.5-cm] dice

5 oz [140 g] fresh or frozen pineapple, cut into cubes

½ cup [120 ml] tomato sauce

½ cup [120 ml] water

3 Tbsp tamari or soy sauce

1 Tbsp sugar

1 recipe Quick Puff Pastry (page 260) or 4 sheets store-bought puff pastry (from two 17.3-oz/490-g packs), thawed and chilled

Ice water for brushing

1 egg white

Preheat the oven to 400°F [200°C]. Line a baking sheet with parchment paper. Put the baking sheet in the refrigerator until ready to use.

In a medium skillet over medium-high heat, warm the olive oil. Add the tempeh and sauté, stirring often, until most of the tempeh is browned on all sides, 7 to 10 minutes. Add the onion and bell pepper and sauté until softened, 7 to 10 minutes. Add the garlic and sauté until fragrant, about 30 seconds more. Add the tomato, pineapple, tomato sauce, water, tamari, and sugar and simmer until the sauce has thickened, 15 to 18 minutes. Remove from the heat and set aside.

Prepare a small bowl of ice water and set aside.

Remove the chilled puff pastry from the refrigerator and transfer to a floured surface. Using a rolling pin, roll out the puff pastry until it's about ⅛ in [4 mm] thick. Put an 8-in [20-cm] round plate, facedown, onto the dough and cut around the edges to create 6 circular dough pieces (you may have to gather the dough scraps and reroll it to use up all the dough). Using a dough scraper or chef's knife, gently lift the dough pieces off the counter, trying to keep their circular shape as much as possible. Transfer all but one of the dough rounds to the refrigerator.

Working with one dough round at a time, brush ice water around the edge. Place a heaping ½ cup [175 g] of the filling in the center of the round and fold one side of the round over the other side to form a crescent shape. Use a fork or your finger to press the edges to seal the pastie. Transfer to the prepared baking sheet. Repeat with the remaining filling and dough.

Freeze the pasties until the dough is very firm, about 30 minutes—this is important so that the butter is chilled or it may melt too fast when baking and cause a pool of butter around your pasties.

Prepare an egg wash by whisking together the egg white and 1 Tbsp water.

Remove the pasties from freezer. Cut three 2-in [5-cm] vent holes in the tops and brush with the egg wash.

Bake until the tops and bottoms are browned, 35 to 40 minutes. Serve immediately or let cool to room temperature. To store, wrap the pasties in aluminum foil, put in an resealable plastic bag, and refrigerate for up to 3 days.

Dried Spiced Pears, Three Ways

You don't need special kitchen equipment to dehydrate food. Your standard oven and a few hours of sticking around the house do the trick! I give you three examples of how I prefer to season my dried pears, so mix and match based on the kind of spices you like! Once dried, store the pears in a resealable bag and throw the bag in your backpack for any adventure. Keep in mind that the flavor is going to be concentrated once the fruit has dried, so a little spice goes a long way.

3 ripe, firm Bartlett pears, unpeeled and thinly sliced

1 Tbsp maple syrup

SWEET PEPPERY ALLSPICE

½ tsp ground allspice

¼ tsp freshly ground black pepper

SPICY CINNAMON

½ tsp ground cinnamon

Pinch of cayenne pepper

GARAM MASALA SPICE

½ tsp garam masala

Preheat the oven to 225°F [110°C]. Line two baking sheets with parchment paper.

Arrange the pear slices in a single layer on the prepared baking sheets. Brush the maple syrup (if using) over both sides of the pears and then sprinkle with the spices from your preferred flavor combination.

Bake, flipping the pears halfway through, until all the moisture is removed and they are brittle instead of spongy, about 3 hours. If your pear slices are thick, you may have to bake them a bit longer.

Remove from the oven and let cool completely. The pears should be completely dried and not chewy at all.

Store in a resealable plastic bag at room temperature for up to 3 months.

Quinoa Wraps with Dill Pesto, Hazelnuts & Apricots

My favorite part about these wraps is that they are vegan, so you don't have to worry about them sitting in your backpack for a couple of hours while you work up an appetite in the woods. These wraps are also brightly flavored, refreshing, and light, so you won't feel like napping after you down one or two. Although they are light, the protein-packed quinoa will keep you going all afternoon. Make sure to rinse the quinoa very well, as it has an outer shell that can be bitter if not removed completely before cooking. Hazelnuts are known to have a bitter skins, too, so don't skip toasting as it will cause the skins to come right off—well worth the extra 10 minutes of prep!

1 cup [180 g] quinoa

2 cups [480 ml] vegetable stock (page 254)

Fine sea salt

½ cup [60 g] hazelnuts

½ cup [15 g] fresh dill leaves

1 small garlic clove, peeled

½ tsp lemon zest

⅓ cup [80 ml] extra-virgin olive oil

Freshly ground black pepper

¼ cup [40 g] diced dried apricots

2 spinach wraps or large flour tortillas

Put the quinoa in a fine-mesh strainer and rinse thoroughly under warm running water for 3 minutes to remove the bitter outer coating.

In a small saucepan over high heat, combine the quinoa, vegetable stock, and ½ tsp salt and bring to a boil. Turn the heat to medium-low, cover, and simmer until most of the stock is absorbed, 15 to 20 minutes. Remove from the heat and let stand, covered, for 5 minutes more. Fluff with a fork and set aside.

Meanwhile, preheat the oven to 275°F [135°C].

Spread out the hazelnuts in a single layer on a baking sheet and bake until toasted, tossing often to keep them from burning, 5 to 7 minutes. Remove from the oven and transfer the hazelnuts to a kitchen towel. Rub the hazelnuts vigorously with the towel until most of the skins have rubbed right off; it should take about 30 seconds or so. Coarsely chop the nuts and transfer half of them to the food processor; set aside the remaining half.

Add the dill, garlic, lemon zest, and olive oil to the food processor and pulse until

a thick pesto forms, about 30 seconds. Season with salt and pepper.

In a large bowl, combine the cooked quinoa, hazelnuts, pesto, and apricots and toss together. Lay the wraps on a work surface and fill each one with 1½ cups [230 g] of the quinoa mixture. Fold in the ends of the wrap and roll tightly. Cover in aluminum foil and store in the refrigerator for up to 12 hours. Unwrap the foil and eat at the most beautiful part of the trail.

Vegan Chocolate-Chip Pumpkin Bread

I really, really, really wanted to include a savory pumpkin bread recipe in this book, but I served it alongside this chocolate pumpkin bread recipe and several of my recipe testers said that this sweet (and vegan!) recipe was just too good to pass up. The bites of coarse salt you taste every once in a while give the perfect savory balance to the not-too-sweet, spiced bread.

2 cups [280 g] whole-wheat flour

1 cup [200 g] packed brown sugar

1 tsp baking soda

1 tsp baking powder

½ tsp fine sea salt

1 tsp ground cinnamon

½ tsp ground nutmeg

½ tsp ground allspice

½ tsp ground cloves

⅔ cup [165 g] pumpkin purée

3 Tbsp maple syrup

2 Tbsp water

½ cup [120 ml] melted coconut oil or extra-virgin olive oil

½ cup [60 g] chopped pecans

½ cup [90 g] dark chocolate chips

¾ cup [105 g] raw pumpkin seeds

⅛ tsp coarse sea salt

Preheat the oven to 350°F [180°C]. Line a 10-in [25-cm] loaf pan with parchment paper.

In a large bowl, whisk together the flour, sugar, baking soda, baking powder, fine sea salt, cinnamon, nutmeg, allspice, and cloves. Make a well in the center of your dry ingredients and add the pumpkin purée, maple syrup, water, and coconut oil into the center. Fold the liquid ingredients into the dry ingredients until just combined. Fold in the pecans, chocolate chips, and ½ cup [70 g] of the pumpkin seeds. (Be careful not to overmix.)

Transfer the batter to the prepared pan and top with the remaining ¼ cup [35 g] of the pumpkin seeds and the coarse sea salt.

Bake until a toothpick inserted into the center of the bread comes out clean, about 1 hour. Transfer to a wire rack and let cool completely. Cut into slices and serve at room temperature. To store, wrap in aluminum foil and store at room temperature for up to 2 days or freeze for up to 2 months.

Peanut Butter Trail Mix Cookies

These cookies are about as easy as they come and chock-full of protein to keep you energized on a long hike. I use peanut butter that has been sweetened with agave, but if you use a version that is completely sugarless, then you may want to add in more maple syrup (depending on how sweet you want these).

1 cup [260 g] creamy peanut butter

¼ cup [60 ml] maple syrup

½ tsp fine sea salt

1 tsp vanilla extract

½ tsp baking soda

½ cup [90 g] of your favorite trail mix (with ingredients such as chocolate chips, chopped pecans, dried cherries, or pumpkin seeds)

Preheat the oven to 350°F [180°C]. Line a baking sheet with parchment paper.

In a large bowl, stir together the peanut butter, maple syrup, salt, vanilla, and baking soda. Fold in the trail mix.

Drop the dough by rounded tablespoons onto the prepared baking sheet, spacing the mounds 2 in [5 cm] apart. Gently press a fork onto the top of each cookie to slightly smash it and make a criss-cross design (the dough will be sticky so try to avoid smearing the cookie).

Bake until the edges begin to brown, about 10 minutes. Let cool completely (they will harden up as they cool). Store in an airtight container at room temperature for up to 5 days.

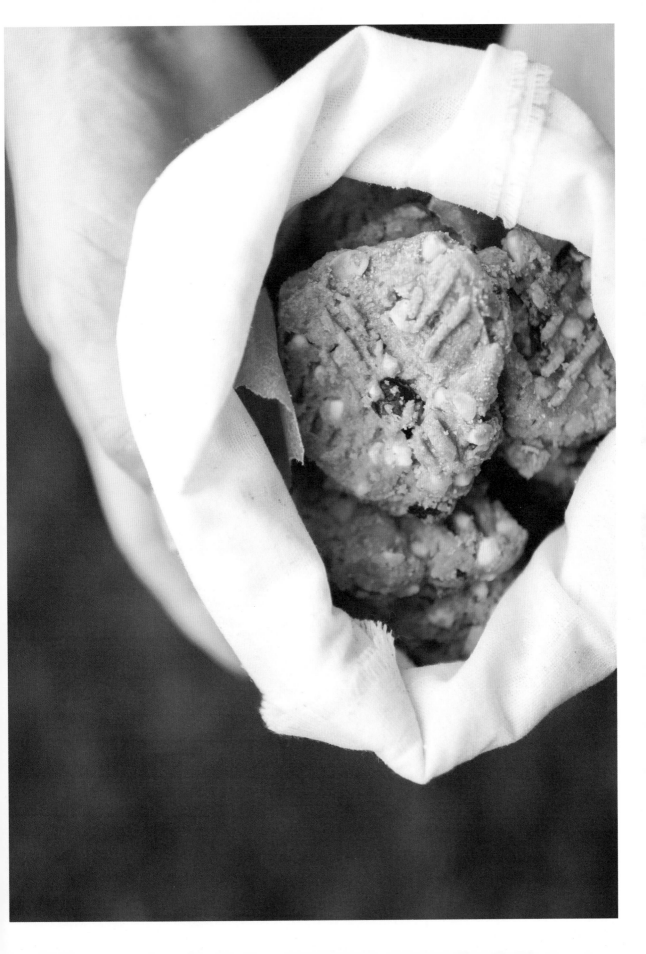

winter

snowed in

recipes to be made while
enjoying the solitude that
arises when the snow piles
too high to wander outside

It is difficult to imagine my life without all four seasons. Some people dream only of the warmth of the sun shining on their faces on Florida beaches, but I also daydream about snow piling so high outside that I get to throw on my warmest pair of long johns, enjoy a cup of coffee by the bay window, fill the kitchen with the smell of freshly baked bread, and spend the entire day slowing down at home.

This chapter is filled with recipes meant to be enjoyed on lazy winter days, when the biggest problem you have to worry about is what color long johns to put on and what recipe you'll tackle next in the kitchen. It also marks the beginning of the winter section; you'll notice this food is substantially heartier than in the rest of the book. The winters are no joke here in the heartland, and you'll find an array of soups, stews, bakes, and a good helping of sweets to perk you up on gray days.

Tomato Curry with Chickpea Dumplings

A few years ago, I came across the original version for this recipe in an international feature in *Saveur* magazine. I've adjusted the recipe over time to create a much quicker variation that can be whipped up as an easy weeknight meal. This recipe has become one of the favorites among my readers, and I've managed to make an even simpler rendition since sharing it on *Vegetarian 'Ventures*. The dumplings are heavily spiced and then steamed in the curry sauce for a delicious alternative to your standard weeknight curry recipe.

1 Tbsp peanut oil, plus ¼ cup [60 ml]

2 tsp coriander seeds

1 tsp yellow mustard seeds

2 serrano chiles, seeded and minced

1 medium yellow onion, minced

1 tsp ground cumin

1½ Tbsp curry powder

½ tsp ground turmeric

Salt

One 1-in [2.5-cm] piece fresh ginger, peeled and grated, or 1 tsp ground ginger

One 28-oz [794-g] can diced tomatoes

1 cup [240 ml] water

1 cup [120 g] chickpea flour

½ cup [25 g] finely chopped fresh cilantro, plus more for garnish

⅓ cup [80 g] Greek yogurt or nondairy yogurt, plus more for garnish

Cooked basmati or long-grain rice for serving

Garlic naan for serving (optional)

In a large skillet over medium heat, warm the 1 Tbsp oil. Add the coriander and mustard seeds and cook until they begin to pop, about 1 minute. Add 1 serrano and half of the onion and sauté until softened, about 5 minutes. Add the cumin, curry powder, turmeric, and ginger, and sauté until the spices begin to toast, about 30 seconds more. Add the tomatoes with juice and the water. Bring to a boil, then turn the heat to medium-low and simmer until thickened, about 10 minutes. Salt to taste.

Meanwhile, in a large bowl, combine the remaining serrano, onion, and ¼ cup [60 ml] oil, the chickpea flour, cilantro, yogurt, and ½ tsp salt and stir together until a thick dough forms.

Drop the dough by rounded tablespoons into the stew. Cover and simmer until the dumplings are cooked all the way through, 5 to 7 minutes. Remove from the heat.

Serve immediately over rice, garnished with cilantro and yogurt, with naan on the side.

Broccoli & Cheddar Frittata

We all know those days that are just too cold to even think straight, let alone get up from under the blanket for more than half-hour intervals. This is probably the easiest recipe in this whole book for those mornings or evenings that you just can't bring yourself to make a big mess in the kitchen. Frittatas are great because they are an effortless way to use up leftover vegetables and usually come together in less than 30 minutes.

8 eggs

1 tsp Dijon mustard

Fine sea salt and freshly ground black pepper

1 Tbsp extra-virgin olive oil

2 cups [180 g] chopped broccoli

2 garlic cloves, minced

½ cup [40 g] shredded cheddar cheese

Preheat the oven to 350°F [180°C].

In a medium bowl, whisk together the eggs, mustard, ½ tsp salt, and ¼ tsp pepper.

In a 10-in [25-cm] oven-safe skillet over medium heat, warm the olive oil. Add the broccoli and garlic and sauté until the broccoli is just beginning to brown, about 3 minutes. Add 3 tsp water, cover, and cook until the broccoli can be easily pierced with a fork, about 2 minutes more. Pour in the egg mixture and sprinkle with the cheese. Cover the pan.

Bake until the egg mixture has completely set, about 10 minutes. Remove the lid and continue to bake until the top begins to brown, 3 to 5 minutes.

Remove from the oven and season with salt and pepper. Cut into wedges and serve warm.

Lager Onion & Lentil Soup

I have such a soft spot for French onion soup, but when I spot it on restaurant menus, it's usually made with beef stock. My version not only ditches the beef stock but also has an extra protein boost from the lentils. It's also a bit Midwestern, as a pale lager beer replaces the white wine you'd find in a traditional French onion soup. Serve with your favorite crusty bread and a hunk of Swiss cheese.

2 Tbsp unsalted butter
4 medium sweet onions, sliced
2 tsp sugar
½ tsp fine sea salt
3 garlic cloves, minced
1 cup [200 g] dried brown lentils
½ Tbsp chopped fresh sage
¼ cup [60 ml] tamari or soy sauce
4 cups [960 ml] water
1 cup [240 ml] pale lager beer
1 bay leaf
Freshly ground black pepper
4 slices whole-wheat baguette
4 to 8 slices Swiss cheese

In a large saucepan over medium heat, melt the butter. Add the onions, sugar, and salt and turn the heat to medium-low. Cook, stirring often to keep the onions from burning, until the onions begin to brown and caramelize, about 40 minutes. The onions should release juices, but if they start to stick to the bottom of the pan, add 1 Tbsp water to the pan to deglaze. Add the garlic and cook until fragrant, 30 seconds more. Add the lentils and sage and cook stirring until toasted, about 1 minute more. Add the tamari, water, beer, and bay leaf. Turn the heat to medium-high and bring the soup to a boil. Turn the heat to low, cover, and simmer until the lentils are soft, about 30 minutes.

Remove from the heat, and season with salt and pepper. Discard the bay leaf.

Preheat the broiler.

Pour the soup into four ramekins or ovenproof bowls. Top each ramekin with a baguette slice, followed by a slice or two of Swiss cheese. Broil until the top has browned and the soup is bubbly, 1 to 2 minutes. Serve immediately.

Baked Pumpkin Risotto with Brown Butter-Sage Bread Crumbs

I love risotto but am not always in the mood to stand over the stove and stir it for more than an hour. This hands-off recipe lets you throw everything into the oven and bake the liquid away. The creamy pumpkin gives this dish an almost cheesy flavor, similar to baked macaroni and cheese. The toasted bread crumb topping gives the final dish an extra crunch. I love serving this dish when having people over for a casual dinner, as the end results feel fancy but I don't have to fuss in the kitchen while guests are around.

Note: Make this recipe vegan by using vegan butter (such as Earth Balance) and swapping nutritional yeast for the Parmesan cheese.

2 Tbsp unsalted butter

1 medium sweet onion, diced

3 garlic cloves, minced

1 Tbsp chopped fresh sage

½ tsp ground nutmeg

1½ cups [300 g] Arborio rice

1 cup [240 ml] white wine

3 cups [720 ml] vegetable stock (page 254)

One 15-oz [425-g] can pumpkin purée

½ cup [15 g] grated Parmesan cheese

Fine sea salt and freshly ground black pepper

TOPPING

4 Tbsp [55 g] unsalted butter, melted

1 cup [140 g] bread crumbs

1 Tbsp chopped fresh sage

Preheat the oven to 350°F [180°C].

In a 10-in [25-cm] Dutch oven with a lid over medium-high heat, melt the butter. Add the onion, sprinkle with salt, and sauté until translucent, about 5 minutes. Add the garlic, sage, and nutmeg and sauté until fragrant, about 30 seconds. Add the rice and sauté until slightly toasted, about 30 seconds. Pour in the wine and let cook until almost all of the liquid has been absorbed, about 1 minute. Add the vegetable stock, pumpkin purée, and Parmesan.

Cover the pan and bake until the rice is soft, 20 to 25 minutes. Remove from the oven and preheat the broiler.

To make the topping: Meanwhile, in a small bowl, combine the butter, bread crumbs, and sage and stir together until the bread crumbs are evenly coated.

Sprinkle the topping over the baked risotto and then broil until the bread crumbs are browned, about 1 minute. (Watch closely because it happens very fast!) Season with salt and pepper and scoop into bowls. Serve immediately.

Whole-Wheat Muesli Bread

There is nothing like letting the smell of fresh baked bread fill your house. I love spending lazy Sunday afternoons making bread that will be my breakfast for the following week. This recipe is filled with all the essentials you would throw into muesli: dried fruit, seeds, and oats. The wonderful mess of delicious muesli ingredients speckle the loaves for a perfectly textured bread.

One 1¼-oz [7 g] packet active dry yeast

1 tsp granulated sugar

1½ cups [360 ml] warm water (110°F to 115°F/43°C to 45°C)

½ cup [120 ml] whole milk

2 Tbsp honey

5 Tbsp [75 g] unsalted butter, melted

2½ cups [350 g] whole-wheat flour

2 cups [280 g] bread flour

1 tsp fine sea salt

1 cup [100 g] old-fashioned rolled oats, plus 2 Tbsp for topping

¼ cup [40 g] chopped dried apricots

¼ cup [30 g] chopped almonds

¼ cup [35 g] dried cherries, chopped

¼ cup [35 g] raw pumpkin seeds, chopped

In a small bowl, stir together the yeast, sugar, and warm water and let stand until foamy, about 5 minutes. Whisk in the milk, honey, and 4 Tbsp [55 g] of the melted butter. Add both flours, the salt, and 1 cup [100 g] of the oats and stir together with a wooden spoon until a sticky dough forms. Transfer the dough to a floured surface and knead in the apricots, almonds, cherries, and pumpkin seeds until the dough is slightly elastic, 5 to 7 minutes. Transfer the dough to an oiled bowl, cover with a kitchen towel, and let rise in a warm spot until doubled, about 1 hour.

Punch down the dough, divide it into two equal pieces, and form into balls. Flour a baking sheet and place the dough balls on the baking sheet. Cover with a kitchen towel and let rise until almost doubled again, about 30 minutes more.

Preheat the oven to 400°F [200°C].

Brush the loaves with the remaining 1 Tbsp melted butter and scatter 1 tablespoon oats over each loaf.

Bake, rotating the baking sheet halfway through, until the tops are browned and a toothpick inserted into each center comes out clean, 40 to 50 minutes.

Let cool completely before slicing. Store at room temperature for up to 3 days or wrap in aluminum foil and freeze for up to 3 months.

Chocolate Gingerbread Cookie Bars

These gingerbread bars are a mix between gingerbread cut-out cookies and brownies. You can serve them without frosting with your afternoon tea, or frost them to create a sweeter, more festive version that's worth sharing with friends for dessert.

1 cup [220 g] unsalted butter

½ cup [160 g] molasses

1 cup [200 g] packed light brown sugar

½ tsp vanilla extract

3 eggs

1½ tsp ground ginger

1 Tbsp ground cinnamon

½ tsp fine sea salt

½ tsp ground cloves

¼ cup [20 g] Dutch-process cocoa powder

1¾ cups [245 g] all-purpose flour

½ cup [90 g] semisweet chocolate chips

FROSTING

2 oz [55 g] cream cheese, at room temperature

4 Tbsp [55 g] unsalted butter, at room temperature

3½ Tbsp eggnog

½ Tbsp rum (optional)

¾ cup [90 g] powdered sugar

Ground cinnamon for dusting

Preheat the oven to 350°F [180°C]. Line a 9-by-13-in [23-by-33-cm] baking pan with parchment paper.

In a medium saucepan over medium heat, melt the butter. Remove from the heat and whisk in the molasses, brown sugar, and vanilla. Let cool for 5 minutes and then whisk in the eggs.

In a small bowl, whisk together the ginger, cinnamon, salt, cloves, cocoa powder, and flour. Make a well in the center of the dry ingredients and pour the molasses mixture into the center. Gradually stir the molasses mixture into the dry ingredients until combined. Fold in the chocolate chips. Pour the batter into the prepared baking pan.

Bake until the center is set, about 25 minutes. Let cool completely.

To make the frosting: Meanwhile, in the bowl of a stand mixer fitted with the whisk attachment, beat the cream cheese and butter on medium speed until completely smooth, about 1 minute. With the mixer running, slowly pour in the eggnog and rum (if using) and beat just until combined. Turn the speed to low, slowly pour in the powdered sugar and beat until a thick frosting forms, about 3 minutes.

Spread the glaze over the gingerbread with a spatula or offset knife and dust with cinnamon. Let stand until the glaze begins to harden, about 10 minutes. Cut into squares and serve.

holiday hosting

elegant and impressive recipes
to serve up to the whole family
at your next gathering

My family is scattered all over the country, from Chicago to Denver to the southern tip of Florida. This means that winter holidays like Thanksgiving and Christmas are big deals, since these are the few occasions that we all come together each year. Thanksgiving and Christmas are the only times when we have a formal feast in the dining room that lasts for hours as we go from appetizers to the main meal to dessert to a strong cup of coffee to lingering around the empty table with one last glass of wine. Throughout the day, food is the centerpiece and a foundation for bringing us all together.

Although I love sitting down for these big feasts, I enjoy preparing for them just as much. The prep work is when I get to spend one-on-one time with my mother as we work out a menu and then dive into several days of cooking. The menu changes every year, as we both love trying new recipes, but you'll find a few favorites in this chapter that have appeared on our table time and again. This chapter ranges from Creamy Sage Gravy (page 217) to delicious vegetarian mains like Caramelized Onion & Fennel Tart (page 224) to rich Mocha Pudding Cups (page 226).

Cranberry Molasses Mulled Wine

Mulled wine is a warm drink usually made with red wine and a handful of mulling spices. I grew up with a German version called glühwein, but countries all over the world have their own version. Mulled wine is an essential in our home during the freezing winter months as it warms the chilled body while also being delicious and festive. This version's secret ingredient is molasses, which is the perfect sweet counterpart to the bright orange zest and tart red wine.

Zest from 1 orange, ¼ cup [60 ml] fresh orange juice, plus orange slices for garnish

2 Tbsp fresh lemon juice

2 green cardamom pods

6 cloves

6 allspice berries

10 black peppercorns

2 cinnamon sticks

¼ cup [50 g] sugar

¼ cup [80 g] molasses

One 750-ml bottle dry red wine

⅓ cup [80 ml] cranberry juice

In a medium saucepan over medium-high heat, combine the orange zest, orange juice, lemon juice, cardamom, cloves, allspice, peppercorns, cinnamon sticks, sugar, molasses, wine, and cranberry juice. As soon as the wine begins to simmer, turn the heat to low and stir until the sugar dissolves. Cover and simmer so the spices can meld into the wine, about 30 minutes. Strain through a fine-mesh sieve, discarding the spices, and serve warm in your favorite mugs. Garnish each serving with an orange slice.

Creamy Sage Gravy

This is the only recipe in this book for which I will encourage you to use dried herbs instead of fresh. Dried sage will result in a silky smooth gravy, perfect for biscuits or serving alongside Thanksgiving dishes. This recipe can easily be made vegan by substituting nondairy butter and unsweetened plain nondairy milk, but watch the gravy closely, as it may thicken sooner or take a bit longer since nondairy milk brands have different consistencies.

¼ cup [35 g] all-purpose flour

3 Tbsp nutritional yeast

2 cups [480 ml] whole milk or unsweetened nondairy milk

2 tsp dried sage

Fine sea salt and freshly ground black pepper

1 Tbsp unsalted butter or nondairy butter

In a small saucepan over medium-high heat, whisk together the flour, nutritional yeast, milk, sage, ½ tsp salt, and ½ tsp pepper. Once simmering, add the butter and turn the heat to medium-low. Whisk continuously until a thick gravy forms, 7 to 10 minutes.

Remove from the heat and season with salt and pepper. Serve immediately.

Everything Spiced "Cheddar Cheese" Ball

Pull this out at your next event, and no one will notice there isn't any cheese in it. This "cheese ball" gets its cheesy flavor from nutritional yeast and its yellow tone from turmeric and paprika. Onion and garlic powders in the cheese mixture and a coating of seeds are reminiscent of the flavors of an everything bagel.

To make a salty-sweet appetizer instead, swap in 7 oz [200 g] macadamia nuts for the cashews, omit the garlic and onion powder, and swap in 1 Tbsp each of chopped cranberries and chopped pistachios.

10 oz [280 g] raw cashews

1 Tbsp sesame seeds

1 Tbsp poppy seeds

1 Tbsp nutritional yeast

1 tsp fresh lemon juice

1 Tbsp extra-virgin olive oil

½ tsp fine sea salt

¼ tsp ground turmeric

½ tsp smoked paprika

1 tsp garlic powder

½ tsp onion powder

Crackers or sliced vegetables for serving

Put the cashews in a large bowl and cover with cold filtered water. Transfer to the refrigerator and soak for at least 2 hours and up to 8 hours.

In a dry small skillet over medium heat, toast the sesame seeds, stirring often, until they start to brown, 3 to 5 minutes. Remove from the heat and transfer to a small plate. Stir in the poppy seeds and set aside.

Drain and rinse the cashews. In a food processor, combine the soaked nuts, nutritional yeast, lemon juice, olive oil, salt, turmeric, paprika, garlic powder, and onion powder and process until a smooth paste forms, 1 to 2 minutes.

Using your hands, shape the dough into a ball and roll the ball in the seed mixture until it's completely coated on all sides. Transfer to a plate, cover with plastic wrap, and refrigerate at least 1 hour or up to 2 days.

Serve at room temperature with crackers or vegetables.

Caramelized Cranberry & Brie Rolls

I have a similar recipe for caramelized cranberry and brie pull-apart bread on my blog, and it's one of the most popular recipes I've ever developed. Every Thanksgiving, friends and family send pictures of themselves baking these rolls, now a staple in their household. I went ahead and morphed that recipe into rolls so it feels even more appropriate for the holidays.

If you're not a fan of Brie, use another creamy cheese you love, but make sure to double-check the label to guarantee that it's vegetarian (see more about this on page 12).

1¼ tsp active dry yeast

¼ cup [60 ml] warm water (110°F to 115°F/43°C to 45°C)

1 cup [240 ml] whole milk

4 Tbsp [55 g] unsalted butter

3 Tbsp granulated sugar

1½ tsp fine sea salt

1 egg, at room temperature

3½ cups [490 g] all-purpose flour

FILLING

6 oz [170 g] fresh cranberries

½ cup [100 g] packed brown sugar

1 Tbsp fresh lemon juice

1 Tbsp unsalted butter

4 oz [115 g] Brie cheese, cut into 36 cubes

2 Tbsp unsalted butter, melted

In a small bowl, stir together the yeast and warm water and let stand until foamy, about 5 minutes.

Meanwhile, in a small saucepan over medium heat, combine the milk and butter and cook until the butter melts, about 2 minutes. Pour the milk mixture into the bowl of a stand mixer fitted with the paddle attachment. Add the sugar and salt and beat on medium speed until combined. With the mixer running, slowly pour in the yeast mixture and the egg and beat just until combined, then slowly add the flour and beat just until a soggy dough forms.

Remove the paddle and attach the dough hook. Knead on medium-high speed until an elastic dough forms, 3 to 4 minutes.

Oil a large bowl. Transfer the dough to the bowl, cover with a kitchen towel, and let rise in a warm spot until doubled, about 1½ hours.

Continued

To make the filling: Meanwhile, in a small saucepan over medium heat, combine the cranberries, brown sugar, lemon juice, and butter. Cook, stirring often, until most of the cranberries have burst and the consistency is that of chunky jam, 7 to 10 minutes. Remove from the heat and let cool.

Preheat the oven to 350°F [180°C]. Generously grease a 9-by-13-in [23-by-33-cm] baking dish.

Divide the dough into four equal pieces and let three of the pieces rest in the covered bowl. Place one piece of dough on a floured surface and divide into three equal pieces and then divide those pieces into another three equal pieces for a total of nine pieces. Roll the dough into a 3-in [7.5-cm] round and place 1 tsp filling and a piece of Brie in the center of the round. Pull all the sides of the dough toward the center to seal the filling and put the dough ball onto the prepared baking dish, seam-side down.

Continue to make the rolls with the remaining dough and filling. Cover the rolls with a kitchen towel and let rise in a warm place until almost doubled, about 30 minutes. Brush 1 Tbsp of the melted butter over the rolls.

Bake until the tops are browned, about 35 minutes. Remove from the oven, brush the tops with the remaining 1 Tbsp melted butter and transfer to a rack to cool slightly. Serve warm.

Roasted Vegetable & Polenta Stacks

These vegetable stacks are not only visually stunning but beyond simple to whip up! Choose vegetables that are all about the same width so that they will easily stack. You are also welcome to swap in any other round vegetable that you'd like. Thick zucchini or eggplant would be delicious if making this dish in the summer.

One 18-oz [510-g] tube precooked polenta, cut into ½-in [12-mm] rounds

1 small white onion, cut into ½-in [12-mm] slices

2 golden beets, peeled and cut into ½-in [12-mm] slices

1 red beet, peeled and cut into ½-in [12-mm] slices

1 medium sweet potato, unpeeled and cut into ½-in [12-mm] slices

2 Tbsp extra-virgin olive oil

1 tsp fine sea salt

Pinch of freshly ground black pepper

SAUCE

3 Tbsp unsalted butter

3 Tbsp all-purpose flour

1 bay leaf

2 cups [480 ml] whole milk

One 2-inch [5-cm] rosemary sprig

1 tsp ground nutmeg

Fine sea salt and freshly ground black pepper

Preheat the oven to 425°F [220°C]. Line two baking sheets with parchment paper.

Arrange the polenta and onion in the center of the prepared baking sheets and the beets and sweet potatoes around the edges. Arrange the vegetables in a single layer, being careful not to overcrowd them. Brush the olive oil on both sides of the polenta and vegetables and sprinkle with the salt and pepper.

Bake, flipping halfway through, until the vegetables are easily pierced with a fork, about 30 minutes. After 20 minutes, check the vegetables often to keep them from burning, removing any that have started to get too brown (most likely the onions).

To make the sauce: Meanwhile, in a medium saucepan over medium heat, whisk together the butter and flour until butter is melted and a thick roux has formed. Add the bay leaf, milk, and rosemary and use a whisk to incorporate the milk into the roux. Bring to a boil over medium-high heat, then turn the heat to medium-low and whisk constantly until the sauce is thick enough to coat the back of a spoon, 5 to 7 minutes. Remove from the heat and discard the rosemary and bay leaf. Whisk in the nutmeg and season with salt and pepper.

Stack a mix of eight vegetable and polenta rounds, using the larger ones toward the bottom. Drizzle with the sauce and serve right away.

Caramelized Onion & Fennel Tart with Rosemary Crust

This filling tart is hearty enough to be the main meal at your next holiday gathering. The dough can be made up to three days ahead and refrigerated, wrapped in parchment paper, until you're ready to roll it out. The caramelized onion-fennel mixture can also be made a day in advance, so you just have to assemble the components and pop the tart in the oven on the day you want to eat it. Slice the onions and fennel as thinly as possible; they'll cook faster. Check them often while caramelizing, as the thickness of your slices will determine cooking time.

CRUST

1¼ cups [175 g] all-purpose flour

½ tsp salt

½ tsp sugar

1 Tbsp finely chopped fresh rosemary

½ cup [110 g] cold unsalted butter, cut into small cubes

1½ Tbsp ice water

1 Tbsp extra-virgin olive oil

3 medium red onions, very thinly sliced

1 fennel bulb, cored and very thinly sliced

Fine sea salt

1 tsp maple syrup

1 Tbsp balsamic vinegar

3 eggs

1½ tsp finely chopped fresh rosemary

½ cup [120 ml] whole milk

Freshly ground pepper

To make the crust: In a food processor, combine the flour, salt, sugar, and rosemary and pulse just to combine. Add the butter and pulse until a crumbly dough forms. With the food processor running, slowly pour in the ice water and process until the dough begins to form a ball. With your hands, gather the loose dough, then shape into a ball on a floured surface and flatten into a disk. Cover in parchment paper or plastic wrap and refrigerate for at least 30 minutes or up to 3 days.

Preheat the oven to 350°F [180°C]. Grease a 9-in [23-cm] pie pan.

Transfer the dough to a floured surface. Using a rolling pin, roll out the dough into a 10-in [25-cm] circle and transfer to the prepared pie pan. Poke the crust all over with a fork.

Bake just until the crust begins to brown, about 15 minutes. Let cool completely.

Meanwhile, in a large saucepan over medium heat, warm the olive oil. Add the onions, fennel, and ½ tsp salt, cover, and cook, stirring often to keep the onions from burning, until onions begin to brown and caramelize, about 40 minutes. The onions should release juices, but if they start to stick to the bottom of the pan, add 1 Tbsp water to the pan to deglaze. Add the maple syrup and balsamic vinegar and sauté until the liquid is completely absorbed, about 5 minutes more. Transfer the caramelized onions to the tart crust and spread evenly on the bottom.

In a small bowl, whisk together the eggs, rosemary, milk, ½ tsp salt, and ⅛ tsp pepper. Pour the egg mixture over the onion mixture. Bake until the top browns and the center sets, about 35 minutes. Cut into wedges and serve warm.

Mocha Pudding Cups with Salted Chocolate Meringue

When I was a little girl, my dad would make pudding as a special weeknight treat. He made it from a box, but, even so, he would make a loud and excited announcement to the whole house to gather around in the kitchen when it was ready. Because of these moments, I'm declaring pudding to be our family dessert (also because root beer floats just don't have a place at the holiday table no matter how much I wish they could). I'm reaching for a new tradition because my Grandma Rosemary's specialty was a murky, neon, molded Jell-O, with speckles of unidentifiable fruit swirled through it. I have no idea how I would ever make that molded Jell-O recipe vegetarian, and I'm not too eager to try it anyway.

This pudding has a very strong coffee flavor, so make sure your friends are coffee fans before serving it, or reduce the amount of instant coffee for a milder coffee flavor. If preparing this for a fancy occasion, be sure to use the meringues; they are a gorgeous and delicious touch. For a weeknight treat, skip the meringue and pull out your favorite whipped cream instead.

PUDDING

¼ cup [50 g] granulated sugar

2 Tbsp cornstarch

1 Tbsp instant coffee granules

½ Tbsp Dutch-process cocoa powder

2 cups [480 ml] whole milk

½ cup [90 g] semisweet chocolate chips

1 Tbsp unsalted butter

1 tsp vanilla extract

⅛ tsp fine sea salt

MERINGUES

½ cup [60 g] powdered sugar

¼ cup [20 g] Dutch-process cocoa powder

4 egg whites, at room temperature

¼ tsp cream of tartar

½ cup [100 g] granulated sugar

Coarse sea salt for sprinkling

To make the pudding: In a medium saucepan, whisk together the granulated sugar, cornstarch, instant coffee, and cocoa powder. Whisk in the milk and set the saucepan over medium heat. Cook, continuously whisking, until the mixture simmers, thickens, and is able to coat the back of a spoon, 8 to 10 minutes. Remove from the heat and add the chocolate chips, butter, vanilla, and salt, whisking until the chocolate melts and everything is evenly combined. Divide the pudding evenly among six ramekins. Cover the puddings with aluminum foil (to avoid a film from forming on the top) and refrigerate for at least 2 hours or up to 2 days.

Continued

To make the meringues: Preheat the oven to 225°F [110°C]. Line a baking sheet with parchment paper.

In a small bowl, sift together the powdered sugar and cocoa powder, then set aside.

In the bowl of a stand mixer fitted with the whisk attachment, whisk the egg whites and cream of tartar on high speed until soft peaks form. With the mixer running, slowly pour in the granulated sugar and whisk until glossy and stiff peaks form. Slowly pour in the cocoa mixture and whisk just until combined.

Spoon the meringue into a piping bag fitted with a #5 tip or a large resealable plastic bag with one corner snipped. Using a spiraling motion, pipe eight 2-in [5-cm] circles onto the prepared baking sheet.

Bake for 1 hour, then turn off the oven and let the meringues remain in the oven until completely dry on the top and bottom, about 15 minutes. Remove from the oven, sprinkle with coarse sea salt, and cool completely.

Place the 6 best-looking meringue cookies on top of each pudding. Serve immediately, with the remaining meringues on the side.

Stollen Cookies

Stollen is a boozy German fruitcake that's oftentimes rolled in powdered sugar and served around Christmastime. My Grandma Betty once told me that they would make stollen for Christmas when she was a kid, and it was one of the only times (aside from when they'd make sauerkraut) that her dad would help out in the kitchen since it's so much work. She now buys stollen from a bakery every holiday season instead of making them. I created these cookies to achieve the same rich flavor via a much simpler process. These shortbread cookies aren't yeasted and don't keep for months, but their almondy flavor studded with boozy fruit shines.

½ cup [70 g] golden raisins

¼ cup [40 g] apricots, diced into raisin-size pieces

¼ cup [35 g] dried cherries

¼ cup [60 ml] rum

1 cup [220 g] unsalted butter, at room temperature, plus 2 Tbsp, melted

1 cup [120 g] powdered sugar

½ tsp orange zest

½ tsp vanilla extract

1 tsp almond extract

2 cups [280 g] all-purpose flour

¼ tsp baking powder

⅛ tsp fine sea salt

⅛ tsp ground nutmeg

⅛ tsp ground allspice

⅛ tsp ground ginger

In a small resealable plastic bag, combine the raisins, apricots, cherries, and rum. Shake the bag around until the dried fruit is evenly coated. Let sit at room temperature about 30 minutes, shaking the bag every few minutes. Drain the dried fruit and reserve the rum for another use.

Meanwhile, in the bowl of a stand mixer fitted with the paddle attachment, beat the 1 cup [220 g] butter, ¾ cup [90 g] powdered sugar, and orange zest on medium speed until combined and a light batter has formed, about 3 minutes. Add the vanilla and almond extract and beat just until combined.

In a small bowl, whisk together the flour, baking powder, salt, nutmeg, allspice, and ginger. With the mixer running on low speed, slowly pour the dry ingredients into the butter-sugar mixture and beat just until blended. Fold in the dried fruit.

Divide the dough into two equal pieces and roll into two 7-in [17-cm] logs. Wrap both logs in wax paper and refrigerate for at least 4 hours or up to 2 days.

Continued

Preheat the oven to 350°F [180°C]. Line two baking sheets with parchment paper.

Cut the logs into ½-in [12-mm] slices and transfer to the prepared baking sheets.

Bake until the edges just begin to brown, 10 to 12 minutes. Remove from the oven and let cool slightly.

Place the remaining 2 Tbsp melted butter and ¼ cup [30 g] powdered sugar in two separate shallow bowls.

Roll the round edges of the cookies in the melted butter and then roll in the powdered sugar. Transfer to a wire rack and let cool completely. These cookies keep in an airtight container at room temperature for up to 1 week.

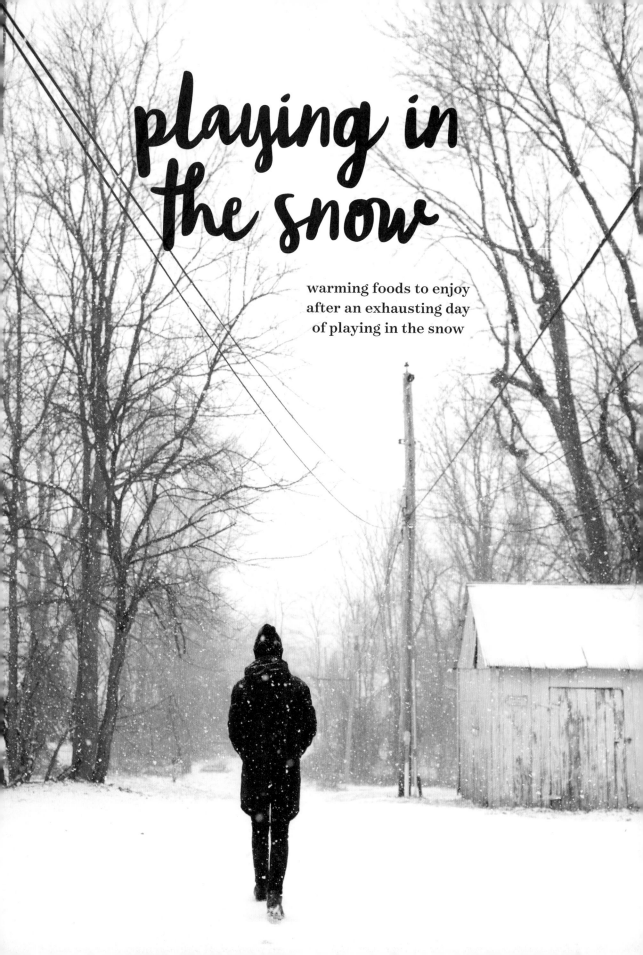

playing in the snow

warming foods to enjoy
after an exhausting day
of playing in the snow

Once it's going to be snowy for the foreseeable future, it's time to throw on a pair of snow pants, an oversize waterproof coat, clunky boots, and get out there to enjoy it! Growing up, my brother and I spent most of our snow day's ice-skating on the lake behind our house or on our family snowmobiles. When we'd return home, exhausted and chilled, my mom would have piping hot chili in mugs waiting for us.

Nowadays I'm the one preparing food after an icy outdoor adventure, but the menu stays the same. In this chapter you will find recipes ranging from hearty Three-Bean Chocolate Chili (page 240) to Chicago-Style Deep-Dish Loaded Veggie Pizza (page 246) to warm Black Bean & Sweet Potato Enchiladas (page 249).

Sledding and ice-skating are my favorite winter activities, but there is always cross-country skiing, snowmobiling, and cold-weather hiking, so get out there and enjoy before the snow melts!

Ricotta, Kale & Fire-Roasted Tomato Quinoa Casserole

This casserole relies on quinoa to create a slightly dense, protein-packed filling. Lean on canned tomatoes in this recipe if fresh ones are terribly out of season (look for a canned variety for which the tomatoes have been packed within hours of picking since they will be the freshest). I love making this dish for dinner on Sunday nights and then reheating the leftovers for the next few days for healthful and quick lunches.

1 cup [180 g] quinoa

½ tsp extra-virgin olive oil, plus 1 Tbsp

2 cups [480 ml] vegetable stock (page 254)

½ tsp fine sea salt

1 medium yellow onion, diced

1 garlic clove, minced

One 14.5-oz [411-g] can fire-roasted diced tomatoes

2 cups [30 g] packed kale, chopped small

1 Tbsp fresh thyme leaves

2 cups [480 g] whole-milk ricotta

½ cup [15 g] grated Parmesan cheese

Fine sea salt and freshly ground black pepper

Put the quinoa in a fine-mesh strainer and rinse thoroughly under warm running water for 3 minutes to remove the bitter outer coating.

In a small saucepan over medium heat, warm the ½ tsp olive oil. Add the quinoa and cook, stirring often, until toasted, about 1 minute. Add the vegetable stock and salt and bring to a boil. Turn the heat to low, cover, and simmer for 15 minutes. Remove from the heat and let stand, covered, for 5 minutes. Fluff with a fork and set aside.

Preheat the oven to 350°F [180°C].

In a large sauté pan over medium heat, warm the remaining 1 Tbsp olive oil. Add the onion and sauté until softened, 5 to 7 minutes. Add the garlic and sauté until fragrant, about 30 seconds. Add the tomatoes with juice and kale and sauté until the tomato liquid evaporates, 3 to 5 minutes. Remove from the heat and fold in the thyme, ricotta, and half of the Parmesan.

Transfer the tomato-kale mixture to a 9-in [23-cm] square baking pan and sprinkle with the remaining Parmesan.

Bake until the Parmesan begins to brown, about 20 minutes. Remove from the oven and let cool slightly. Season with salt and pepper and serve warm.

Chocolate Chai Concentrate

Spicier than it is sweet, this concentrate is the perfect winter warmer to have on hand during cold months. It makes whipping up a delicious hot drink, packed with nutrients, as quick as preparing packaged cocoa.

I really love the subtle tropical flavor that coconut milk adds, but any type of milk will work. You can also make a delicious iced chai version by skipping the reheating step and adding ice. Add more maple syrup or sweetener of choice after mixing with milk and tasting.

4 cinnamon sticks

12 green cardamom pods

9 cloves

2 vanilla beans, split lengthwise

2 whole star anise

8 black peppercorns

One 1-in [2.5-cm] piece fresh ginger, peeled and sliced

2 Tbsp Dutch-process cocoa powder

2 Tbsp maple syrup, plus more for serving

3 cups [720 ml] water

3 black tea bags or 5 tsp loose-leaf black tea

Your preferred milk, such as whole milk or nondairy milk, for serving

Star anise, for garnish

In a small saucepan over medium heat, combine the cinnamon, cardamom, cloves, vanilla beans, star anise, peppercorns, ginger, cocoa, maple syrup, and water and bring to a boil. Turn the heat to low and simmer, stirring occasionally, until the cocoa dissolves. Cover and simmer until very fragrant, about 15 minutes more. Remove from the heat, then add the tea bags and let steep, covered, about 5 minutes.

Remove the tea bags and strain through a fine-mesh sieve into a glass jar with a lid. Discard the solids and refrigerate in an airtight container for up to 5 days.

To serve, warm equal parts of concentrate and milk in a saucepan over medium-low heat, stirring often, until hot, about 5 minutes. Add more maple syrup to taste, if needed. Serve warm, with a star anise pod.

Purple Potatoes Poached in Dill Cream Sauce

This simple-yet-indulgent recipe is a favorite for when I am feeling chilled to the bone. Rich and full of comforting flavors, it's one of the main recipes my body craves when we are experiencing below-freezing temperatures. Like scalloped potatoes, it's baked in the oven, but the potatoes are halved rather than sliced for a dramatic presentation. Serve alongside an egg dish, Caramelized Onion & Fennel Tart (page 224), or with a hearty casserole.

Small purple potatoes give this dish extra color that complements the green dill nicely. If you are having trouble finding them, then small red potatoes will also work just fine.

1 lb [455 g] small purple potatoes, scrubbed and halved crosswise

1¼ cups [300 ml] heavy cream

2 garlic cloves, minced

Fine sea salt

Freshly cracked black pepper

1 Tbsp fresh chopped dill, plus more for garnish

Preheat the oven to 350°F [180°C].

Arrange the potatoes, cut-side down, in the bottom of a 9-in [23-cm] round or square baking dish, putting the smaller halves toward the center and larger potatoes toward the edge.

In a small bowl, whisk together the cream, garlic, 1 tsp salt, ½ tsp pepper, and dill. Pour the cream mixture over the potatoes, making sure that the tops are all coated (the cream will come just about halfway up the potatoes). Cover with aluminum foil.

Bake for 40 minutes. Remove the aluminum foil and bake until the cream bubbles and begins to turn brown in spots, about 10 minutes more. Remove from the oven, season with salt and pepper, and let cool slightly before serving. Spoon potato halves onto serving plates and serve with more fresh dill.

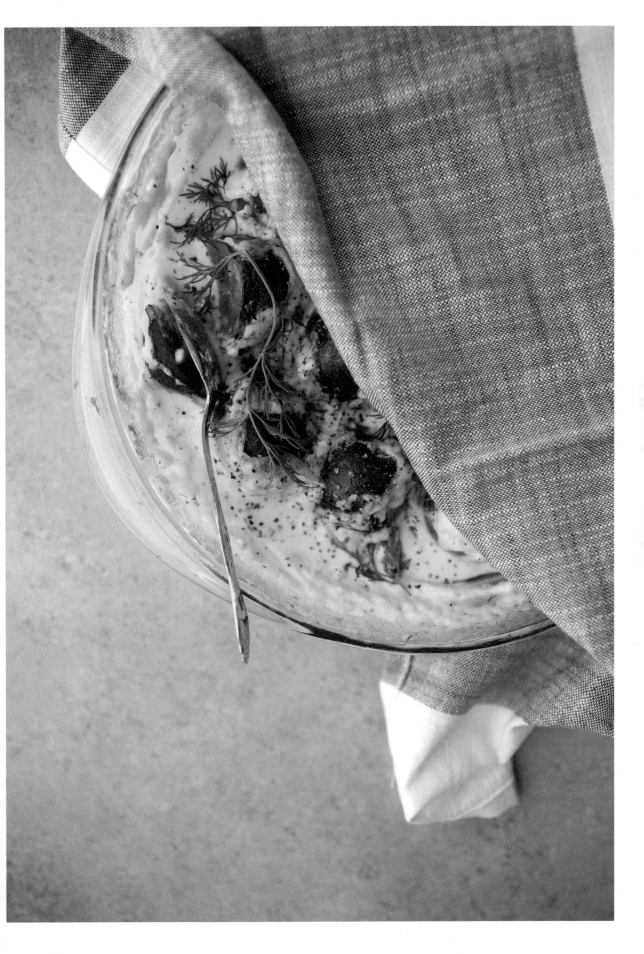

Three-Bean Chocolate Chili

When I was first learning to cook, a friend and I would get together once a week and navigate our way through two or three recipes together. We were still learning how to read a recipe, and it usually took us twice as long as the recipe said it should, but it ended up being the fundamental excitement that got me into cooking. We recorded all the recipes that we tried in a notebook and would make all sorts of notes about what worked and didn't. I haven't seen that notebook in years, but the chili recipe we tackled became a staple in my college kitchen, and I soon learned to whip it up from memory.

Each time I prepared the recipe, I tweaked it a bit until I arrived at this version. This big-batch one-pot chili is easy enough for any skill level and is not only chock-full of protein-rich beans but is also loaded with vegetables and spices.

¼ cup [60 ml] extra-virgin olive oil

1 large yellow onion, chopped

1 green bell pepper, seeded, deribbed, and chopped

3 large garlic cloves, minced

2 Tbsp chili powder

1 Tbsp Dutch-process cocoa powder

2 tsp dried oregano

1½ tsp ground cumin

½ tsp cayenne pepper

One 15-oz [425-g] can black beans, drained, or 1½ cups [240 g] cooked beans (page 264)

One 15-oz [425-g] can kidney beans, drained, or 1½ cups [240 g] cooked beans (page 264)

One 15-oz [425-g] can pinto beans, drained, or 1½ cups [240 g] cooked beans (page 264)

One 14.5-oz [411-g] can fire-roasted diced tomatoes

2½ cups [600 ml] vegetable stock (page 254)

1 cup [140 g] frozen corn

Sour cream, shredded cheddar cheese or nutritional yeast, chopped fresh cilantro leaves and/or chopped avocado for serving (optional)

Continued

In a large saucepan over medium heat, warm the olive oil. Add the onion, bell pepper, and garlic and sauté until the vegetables soften and the garlic is fragrant, about 5 minutes. Add the chili powder, cocoa powder, oregano, cumin, and cayenne, stirring to coat, and sauté until fragrant, about 30 seconds more. Add the beans, tomatoes with juice, stock, and corn.

Turn the heat to medium-high, bring to a boil, and then turn the heat to medium-low, cover, and simmer until the vegetables and beans are completely soft, 15 to 20 minutes. Remove the lid and simmer until the chili thickens and most of the liquid has cooked off, about 5 minutes more. Remove from the heat and let cool slightly. Ladle into bowls or mugs. Serve warm and pass sour cream, cheese, cilantro, and/or avocado (if using) around the table. Leftovers will last up to 3 days refrigerated in an airtight container or up to 3 months in the freezer.

Vegan Wild Rice & Potato Chowder

The key to this creamy vegan chowder is the silky cashew cream that gets stirred in toward the end. Since there aren't any herbs in this chowder, season generously with salt and pepper to bring out the flavors of the wild rice and vegetables.

Make sure to check the wild rice often during cooking as the kernels are all different sizes and finish at different times. Also, look for wild rice in the bulk section of your grocery store, where it is usually much cheaper. Serve this chowder along with a fresh baguette to make this a hearty meal that's sure to warm you up on a chilly evening.

1 cup [180 g] wild rice, rinsed

2 Tbsp olive oil

1 medium red onion, diced

4 medium Yukon gold potatoes, unpeeled and finely diced

2 medium carrots, diced

3 celery stalks, diced

Fine sea salt

3 garlic cloves, minced

¼ cup [35 g] all-purpose flour

4 cups [960 ml] vegetable broth

2½ cups [600 ml] water

½ cup [70 g] raw cashews, soaked in water for at least 4 hours

Freshly ground black pepper

In a large saucepan over high heat, bring 3 cups [720 ml] salted water to a boil. Add the wild rice to the boiling water, turn the heat to low, cover, and simmer just until the rice has softened and the kernels puff open, about 40 minutes. Drain and set aside.

Meanwhile, in another large saucepan or stockpot, warm the olive oil over medium heat. Add the onion, potatoes, carrots, celery, and 1 tsp salt and sauté until the vegetables soften, 10 to 12 minutes. Add the garlic and sauté until fragrant, about 30 seconds more. Add the flour and cook, stirring to coat the vegetables with flour, about 30 seconds. Slowly pour in ¼ cup [60 ml] of the vegetable broth, stirring until the flour is absorbed into the broth. Add the remaining 3¾ cups [900 ml] vegetable broth and 2 cups [480 ml] water. Bring to a boil over medium-high heat, then turn the heat to low, cover, and simmer for 30 minutes.

Continued

While the soup is simmering, in a high-speed blender, combine the drained cashews and ½ cup [120 ml] water and blend on high speed until smooth and thin creamy sauce forms, about 45 seconds.

After the soup has simmered for 30 minutes, stir in the wild rice and cashew cream. Simmer, uncovered, until the soup thickens to a chowder consistency, about 10 minutes more. Season with salt and pepper.

Divide the soup among 6 bowls. Serve immediately.

Chicago-Style Deep-Dish Loaded Veggie Pizza

As a kid, my favorite restaurant, hands down, was Gino's East in Chicago. Back then it was in a tiny space that was covered in graffiti. Everything about it was the coolest from a kid's perspective—you got to stand in a line that wrapped around the corner because it was that exclusive, you could (and were encouraged to) write all over the walls, and you got to eat insane amounts of pizza for dinner. What more could a kid want? As an adult, I still wait in line for dinner because their deep-dish pizza is the best I've ever had.

But I no longer live close enough that heading to Gino's on impulse is an option. I first made deep-dish pizza to cure homesickness but began making it often in the winter once I discovered that it's no more effort than making a regular homemade pizza! Make the crust from scratch if you have the time, since the Chicago deep dish I know and love has a cornmeal kick to it and tends to be a little more buttery than any store-bought dough I've come across.

To reduce time for this recipe, make the dough first and then assemble all of your toppings and sauce while it rises. I recommend two springform pans for this recipe, but cake pans will work, too.

One 1¼-oz [7-g] packet active dry yeast

1 tsp sugar plus 1 Tbsp

1¼ cups [300 ml] warm water (110° to 115°F/43° to 45°C)

½ cup [110 g] unsalted butter

3½ cups [490 g] all-purpose flour

½ cup [70 g] coarse cornmeal, plus more for sprinkling

1 tsp fine sea salt

1 lb [455 g] mozzarella cheese, shredded

Optional toppings: thinly sliced green bell pepper, thinly sliced onion, diced cherry tomatoes, sliced button mushrooms, pitted black olives, pineapple chunks, sliced marinated artichoke hearts

1 recipe Basic Tomato Sauce (page 258) or 3 cups [720 ml] store-bought sauce

In a small bowl, stir together the yeast, 1 tsp of the sugar, and ¼ cup [60 ml] of the warm water and let stand until foamy, about 5 minutes.

In a small saucepan over medium heat, combine the remaining 1 cup [240 ml] water and the butter and cook until the butter melts, about 2 minutes.

In the bowl of a stand mixer fitted with the paddle attachment, mix together the flour, cornmeal, salt, and the remaining 1 Tbsp sugar on medium-low speed until combined, about 20 seconds. With the mixer on medium-low speed, slowly add the butter mixture and the yeast mixture and mix until combined. Remove the paddle and attach the dough hook. Knead on medium-high speed until an elastic dough forms, about 5 minutes.

Continued

Oil a large bowl. Transfer the dough to the bowl, cover with a kitchen towel, and let rise in a warm spot until doubled, about 1½ hours.

Line two 9-in [23-cm] springform pans or two 9-in [23-cm] cake pans that are 2 in [5 cm] deep with aluminum foil and sprinkle with cornmeal.

Punch down the dough and transfer it to a floured surface. Divide it into two equal pieces and form into balls. Using a rolling pin, roll out the dough balls into 12-in [30.5-cm] rounds. Transfer the rounds to the prepared pans and press firmly against bottom and sides to keep it in place. Cover again with kitchen towels and refrigerate until completely chilled, about 1 hour.

Preheat the oven to 425°F [220°C].

For each pizza, sprinkle half of the mozzarella over the bottom of the dough, spreading it evenly. Cover with up to ½ cup [75 g] of toppings and then drizzle half of the tomato sauce over the toppings.

Bake until the sauce is bubbly, 25 to 30 minutes. Remove from the oven and let cool for 5 minutes before serving. Cut into wedges and serve. Don't be afraid to use a knife and fork for these pizza slices!

Black Bean & Sweet Potato Enchiladas

These enchiladas have become a weeknight staple in our house. Depending on the amount of time you'd like to invest in this meal, you can make the enchilada sauce from scratch (page 263) or use your favorite store-bought version. Make these vegan by removing the cheddar cheese and adding an extra 1 cup [160 g] of black beans instead.

1½ lb [680 g] sweet potatoes, peeled, sliced into ½-inch [12-mm] strips

One 15-oz [425-g] can black beans, rinsed and drained, or 1½ cups [240 g] cooked beans (page 264)

4 garlic cloves, minced

1½ Tbsp fresh lime juice

One 4-oz [113-g] can fire-roasted green chiles

2 Tbsp chopped fresh cilantro, plus more for garnish

1 Tbsp ground cumin

1½ cups [120 g] shredded mild white cheddar cheese

1 cup [240 ml] Homemade Enchilada Sauce (page 263) or store-bought canned enchilada sauce

5 burrito-size flour tortillas

Cilantro for serving

Preheat the oven to 350°F [180°C].

Fill a pot with 1 in [2.5 cm] of water and bring to a simmer over medium-high heat. Place the sweet potato in a steamer basket and set the basket over the simmering water. Cover and steam until the strips are easily pierced by a knife, 10 to 12 minutes.

In a large bowl, stir together the black beans, garlic, lime juice, green chiles, cilantro, cumin, and 1 cup [80 g] of the cheddar cheese. Set aside.

Pour ½ cup [120 ml] of the enchilada sauce into the bottom of a 9-in [23-cm] square baking dish. Evenly lay ten pieces of sweet potato in line down the center of a tortilla and pour ½ cup [100 g] of the black bean filling over the sweet potatoes. Roll up the tortilla as tightly as possible and transfer to the baking dish. Repeat with the remaining tortillas and filling. Drizzle the remaining ½ cup [120 ml] enchilada sauce over the filled tortillas and sprinkle the remaining ½ cup [40 g] cheese over the top.

Bake until the cheese starts to brown, about 25 minutes. Sprinkle with cilantro and serve warm.

Peppermint Cocoa Truffles

Every December, we travel to Macy's in Chicago to see their famous Christmas tree and pick up a few boxes of Frango mints, which are rich chocolate truffles that are a Chicagoan staple around the holidays. After moving to southern Indiana, I had trouble finding these mint truffles and decided to tackle making my own. This version is rolled in cocoa powder but you can make them more festive by rolling in red or green sugar or sprinkles.

Make sure you have all your ingredients out before starting on this recipe, as you'll need to be quick once the heavy cream starts boiling. The chocolate will look, at first, like it might not whisk well into the butter and cream mixture but just keep whisking, and it will all come together.

½ cup [120 ml] heavy cream

4 Tbsp [55 g] unsalted butter, cut into cubes

12 oz [340 g] semisweet chocolate chips

2 tsp peppermint extract

⅓ cup [25 g] Dutch-process cocoa powder

In a small saucepan over medium heat, bring the heavy cream to a boil. Add the butter and cook, whisking constantly, until melted, about 15 seconds. Add the chocolate and whisk continuously until smooth, about 30 seconds. Remove from the heat and whisk in the peppermint extract. Transfer the chocolate mixture to a shallow bowl, cover, and refrigerate until firm, at least 2 hours or up to 24 hours.

Remove the chocolate mixture from the refrigerator. Put the cocoa powder in a shallow bowl. Use a Tbsp measuring spoon or melon baller to scoop out a heaping Tbsp of the chocolate mixture and roll between the palms of your hands to form a uniform ball. Roll the ball in the cocoa powder until evenly coated and transfer to a serving plate. Continue to make the balls with the remaining chocolate and cocoa.

Serve immediately or transfer to a resealable container and refrigerate for up to 10 days.

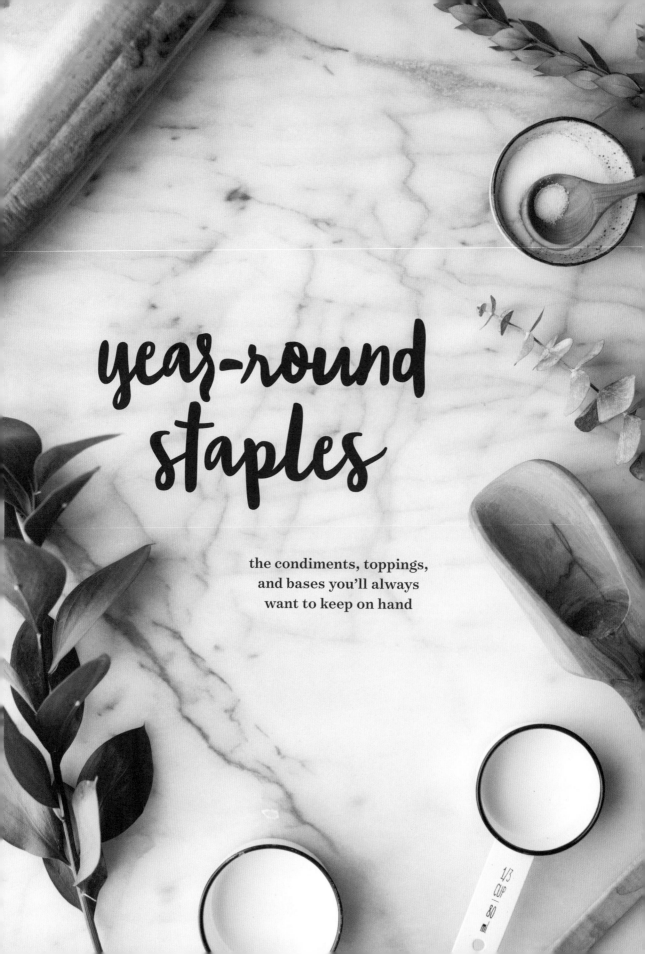

year-round staples

the condiments, toppings, and bases you'll always want to keep on hand

This section is not filled with glamorous recipes that will have your guests raving for days. However, these recipes are the building blocks for your awe-inspiring recipes, the ones your guests go on and on about being so good as they try to put their fingers on what makes them so special. There are all sorts of reasons why making kitchen staples from scratch is beneficial, but my favorite is the extra flavor it gives to dishes. Making your own kitchen staples is also oftentimes cheaper than the store-bought versions and gives you total control over the ingredients so you don't have to worry about any commercial preservatives you can't pronounce.

Homemade Vegetable Stock

If there is one recipe that becomes a staple in your kitchen, make it this one. Vegetable stock is not only simple to make, but it's a great way to utilize leftover vegetable scraps and much cheaper (and tastier!) than relying on store-bought stock. To use up your old vegetable scraps for the stock, just throw them (this includes vegetable ends, herb stems, and so on) into a large resealable freezer bag and stick in the freezer. Once your bag is full, pull it out and follow these instructions.

I freeze my stock in ice-cube trays and just make a note of how much each cube yields (for example, six of my stock cubes equal ½ cup [120 ml]) so I can easily pull out just enough for the recipe I am working on.

5 cups [750 g] vegetable scraps (see the following list) or chopped vegetables

1 bay leaf

8 to 10 black, pink, or green peppercorns

2 garlic cloves, crushed (optional, but recommended)

1 Tbsp tomato paste (optional, but recommended)

In a stockpot, combine the vegetable scraps, bay leaf, peppercorns, garlic, and tomato paste, and add cold water to cover by about 1 in [2.5 cm]. Bring to a boil over high heat. Once boiling, turn the heat to medium-low and simmer for 1 hour.

Strain the vegetable stock through a fine-mesh sieve into a pitcher or large bowl and discard the scraps. Let cool completely.

Store in an airtight container in the refrigerator for up to 5 days and in the freezer for up to 3 months.

Here is a list of vegetables and herbs I'd recommend using in your stock. Be sure to use vegetables that you like so the subtle flavor found in the stock will reflect those flavors.

» Onions, leeks, and scallions (red onion will dye your stock a bit pink but won't mar the flavor)

» Bell peppers

» Eggplant

» Root vegetables (beets will dye the stock purple but won't mar the flavor)

» Mushrooms

» Fresh herbs (basil, sage, rosemary, cilantro, and so on)—this includes the stems!

» Garlic

» Broccoli

» Asparagus

» Fennel

» Celery

» Leafy greens and their stems (kale, chard, and so on)

Bread Crumbs

Making bread crumbs seems like it shouldn't even be a written recipe, but they are certainly a staple for every kitchen and a great way to use up stale or leftover bread. Once you realize how easy it is to whip up your own, you will never rely on the store-bought version again. For everyday use, I save leftover stale bread and bread ends by tossing them into a resealable freezer bag and freezing until needed. When I need bread crumbs, I pull out enough bread ends to fit on a baking sheet and follow this recipe (baking a little longer if necessary if the bread is frozen).

1 lb [455 g] stale bread, cut into large chunks

Preheat the oven to 275°F [135°C].

Spread out the bread chunks in a single layer on the baking sheet. Bake, flipping the bread halfway through, until toasted, about 15 minutes. Remove from the oven.

Transfer the bread to a food processor and process until it has turned into a coarse meal, about 30 seconds. If you don't have a food processor, then you can put bread chunks in a sealed plastic bag and beat with a rolling pin until you are left with mostly coarse crumbs.

Return the bread crumbs to the baking sheet and spread out into a single layer. Bake, stirring halfway through, until browned, about 10 minutes. Remove from the oven. Store in an airtight container in the freezer for up to 3 months.

VARIATIONS:

Parmesan-Italian: Combine ¼ cup [8 g] grated Parmesan cheese, 1 tsp dried oregano, ½ tsp garlic powder, a pinch of fine sea salt, a pinch of freshly ground black pepper with the bread crumbs when returning to the oven.

Black Sesame Rye: Combine ⅓ cup [45 g] black sesame seeds and ½ tsp onion powder with rye bread crumbs when returning to the oven.

Quick Spiced Applesauce

Enjoy this applesauce on warm German Fennel & Sweet Potato Pancakes (page 157), swirled in your morning porridge, or by itself for a quick and nutritious snack. I like leaving the apples in little chunks, but you are welcome to purée the apples with a hand blender for a more traditional applesauce.

1 lb [455 g] apples, cored, peeled, and chopped into 1-in [2.5-cm] pieces

2 Tbsp brown sugar

1 Tbsp unsalted butter

1 tsp ground cinnamon

½ tsp ground nutmeg

3 Tbsp water

In a medium saucepan over medium heat, combine the apples, brown sugar, butter, cinnamon, nutmeg, and water. Cook, stirring, until the butter melts and the apples are coated with the spices, 3 to 5 minutes. Turn the heat to low, cover, and simmer until the apples are easily pierced with a fork, about 20 minutes. Remove from the heat and let cool to room temperature. Store in an airtight container in the refrigerator for up to 10 days.

Basic Tomato Sauce

Making your own sauce from scratch can quickly jazz up a boring night of pasta for dinner. This basic tomato sauce can be made in less than 30 minutes, and you'll have fresh homemade sauce by the time you're done boiling the pasta. This sauce also works great in pizza (page 246) and lasagna.

1 Tbsp extra-virgin olive oil

1 yellow onion, diced

2 garlic cloves, minced

¼ cup [60 ml] red wine (optional)

2 tsp dried Italian herbs or 2 Tbsp chopped fresh Italian herbs (such as oregano, basil, or thyme)

One 28-oz [794-g] can whole tomatoes

1 tsp sugar (optional)

⅛ tsp red pepper flakes (optional)

Fine sea salt and freshly ground black pepper

In a large skillet over medium heat, warm the olive oil. Add the onion and sauté until translucent, about 5 minutes. Add the garlic and sauté until fragrant, about 30 seconds. Add the wine (if using) and herbs and turn the heat to high. Let the wine simmer until almost all the liquid is evaporated, 1 to 3 minutes. Add the tomatoes, sugar (if using), and red pepper flakes (if using). Using your hands or a knife, break apart the tomatoes. Simmer until the sauce thickens and has reached the desired consistency, 8 to 12 minutes. Remove from the heat and season with salt and pepper. Store in an airtight container in the refrigerator for up to 3 days.

Cashew Cream, Four Ways

Cashew cream is a great substitute for creamy cheese when you are looking for a healthful alternative to dairy products. I've listed three variations to help match the recipe into which you're trying to incorporate the cream. The herbed and roasted bell pepper versions are great on pasta or vegan pizza and the sweetened maple is perfect to top any dessert that would benefit from a dollop of whipped cream. Note that the ingredients for the maple syrup and roasted red pepper versions have more liquid, so purèe the cashews with less water and plan on thinning them out slightly once done.

1 cup [140 g] raw cashews, rinsed

⅓ cup [80 ml] filtered water, plus more for soaking

Put the cashews in a bowl and cover with filtered water. Transfer to the refrigerator and soak for at least 3 hours or up to 5 hours.

Drain and rinse the cashews. In a high-speed blender or food processor, combine the soaked nuts and ⅓ cup [80 ml] water and blend until smooth and creamy, about 45 seconds. If the cream is too thick, add more water, 1 Tbsp at a time, until the cream reaches the desired consistency.

Store in an airtight container in the refrigerator for up to 3 days.

VARIATIONS:

Herbed Cashew Cream: Fold 1 tsp chopped fresh oregano, 1 tsp chopped fresh dill, 1 tsp chopped fresh basil, and a pinch of salt into the cashew cream after it's blended.

Roasted Red Pepper Cashew Cream: Add 4 oz [115 g] roasted red bell peppers, drained, to the blender and purée along with cashews.

Maple Cashew Cream: Fold 3 tsp maple syrup and a pinch of salt into the cashew cream after it's blended.

Quick Puff Pastry

Serious pastry enthusiasts may wince at this laid-back recipe for making puff pastry, but it is meant for the everyday baker. This pared-down version can be made in minutes instead of hours, yet it's still flaky and delicious and works anytime pastry dough is called for in this book. (I'd recommend using it for the pasties on page 184 or the Cranberry & Pear Turnover Breakfast Bake on page 147.)

2 cups [280 g] all-purpose flour
¼ tsp fine sea salt
20 Tbsp [275 g] cold unsalted butter, cut into cubes
⅔ cup [160 ml] ice water

In a medium bowl, whisk together flour and salt. Using a pastry blender or your hands, quickly cut the butter into the dough until a coarse dough has formed and all the butter is pea-size or smaller. Make a well in the center of the mixture and pour in the ice water. Fold the dry ingredients, with your hands or a wooden spoon, into the water until a shaggy dough forms.

Transfer the dough (it will feel dry, and that's okay) to a floured surface and knead just until it comes together. Form the dough into a loose square and, using a floured rolling pin, roll out the dough into a rectangle that is at least 12 in [30.5 cm] long. Fold the upper third of the dough over the middle third and then fold the bottom third of the dough over that, similar to folding a business letter. Rotate the dough 45 degrees, flour the top and bottom of the dough, and repeat the process by rolling out the dough into a rectangle and folding over in thirds again. Repeat this process eight times for a total of two complete rotations. If the dough becomes too soft at any point in the rolling process, transfer it to the fridge and refrigerate for 10 minutes before continuing.

Cover the dough in plastic wrap and refrigerate for at least 1 hour or up to overnight before using.

Caramelized Date Barbecue Sauce

This barbecue sauce is sweetened naturally with dates, has a slight tang from the vinegar, and a subtle smokiness from liquid smoke. Use as a condiment with Wild Rice Veggie Sliders (page 136) or your favorite french fries.

1 Tbsp unsalted butter

4 oz [115 g] Medjool dates, pitted and quartered

1 small yellow onion, diced

1 garlic clove, minced

1 tsp smoked paprika

½ tsp red pepper flakes

One 15-oz [425-g] can of tomato sauce

½ cup [120 ml] red wine vinegar

2 Tbsp tomato paste

¼ cup [80 g] molasses

2 Tbsp tamari or soy sauce

2 tsp liquid smoke

Fine sea salt and freshly ground black pepper

In a medium saucepan over medium heat, melt the butter. Add the dates and sauté, stirring frequently, until they are completely softened and start to break down, 8 to 10 minutes. Add the onion and sauté until soft and translucent, about 5 minutes. Add the garlic, paprika, and red pepper flakes and sauté until fragrant, about 30 seconds. Add the tomato sauce, vinegar, tomato paste, molasses, tamari, liquid smoke, ½ tsp salt, and ¼ tsp black pepper. Bring to a simmer and cook, uncovered, until the sauce has thickened, about 20 minutes.

Remove from the heat and let cool for 5 minutes. Use an immersion blender to blend until smooth. Return to medium heat and cook for 5 minutes more.

Remove from the heat and season with salt and pepper. Store in an airtight container in the refrigerator for up to 1 week or in the freezer for up to 3 months.

Homemade Enchilada Sauce

Enchilada sauce was a condiment I grew up with, but I never knew what was in it until I made my own. It's a simple sauce for tacos and perfect for the Black Bean & Sweet Potato Enchiladas (page 249). I don't have much of a tolerance for spicy foods, so this recipe is rather mild, but you are welcome to add more jalapeños if you'd like it spicier.

1½ cups [360 ml] vegetable stock

2 fresh or dried red chiles (such as ancho or guajillo) halved lengthwise and seeded

2 jalapeño chiles

2 Tbsp extra-virgin olive oil

½ medium red onion, diced

2 garlic cloves, chopped

2 large tomatoes, diced

¼ cup [55 g] tomato paste

1 tsp dried oregano

1 tsp ground cumin

Fine sea salt and freshly ground black pepper

Pour the vegetable stock into a small saucepan and bring to a simmer over medium-high heat. Add the red chiles (fresh or dried) and simmer until softened, about 15 minutes. Remove from the heat but don't drain the stock. Set aside.

Char the jalapeños by placing them directly over a gas burner until blackened on all sides (or broil in your oven). Remove from the heat and immediately transfer to a resealable plastic bag. Let steam in the bag for about 15 minutes and then peel the skins right off. Cut in half lengthwise and remove the seeds. Set aside.

In a large saucepan over medium heat, warm the olive oil. Add the onion and garlic and sauté until the onion is translucent, about 7 minutes. Add the tomatoes, tomato paste, red chiles with the vegetable stock, jalapeños, oregano, and cumin and simmer until thickened and liquid has reduced to half, about 10 minutes. Remove from the heat and cool slightly. Transfer to a blender and blend until smooth. Season with salt and pepper.

Store in an airtight container in the refrigerator for up to 4 days or in the freezer for up to 3 months.

Slow-Cooker Beans

This recipe was designed for any type of bean so the cooking time varies based on the size of bean, type, and also how old the bean is. We do a quick boil of the beans before adding to the slow cooker to create a quicker cooking time and also make them more digestible for our systems. I've read that the quick boil beforehand is particularly important for any type of kidney bean, but I do a quick boil for all beans just to make them easier on my digestive system. If making black beans for Mexican cuisine, you can add in dried peppers for additional flavor.

1½ cups dried beans [270 g], soaked overnight in the fridge

1 bay leaf

7 black peppercorns

2 garlic cloves, peeled

Fine sea salt

Place the beans in a medium saucepan and add enough water so to cover by 3 inches (7.5 cm). Bring to a boil over medium-high heat and boil for 2 minutes. Remove from the heat, cover, and let stand for 1 hour. Rinse the beans and transfer to a slow cooker.

Add the bay leaf, peppercorns, garlic, and enough water to cover the beans by 1 in [2.5 cm]. Cover and cook on low for 6 to 8 hours, checking to see if the beans are soft and cooked all the way through after 6 hours. Be prepared to let them cook longer. Once done, drain and season with salt.

Store in an airtight container in the refrigerator for up to 1 week or in the freezer for up to 3 months. To freeze, place in a single layer on a baking sheet and freeze for 30 to 60 minutes, then transfer to a resealable plastic freezer bag.

Savory Granola

Enjoy this savory granola in a salad (perhaps the Green Salad with Savory Granola & Avocado-Lime Dressing on page 28), over yogurt, or by itself as an afternoon snack.

1 cup [100 g] old-fashioned rolled oats

½ cup [70 g] shelled pistachios

½ cup [70 g] raw pumpkin seeds

1 tsp chopped fresh rosemary

¼ tsp fine sea salt

⅛ tsp freshly ground black pepper

1 egg white, whisked for 30 seconds

Preheat the oven to 350°F [180°C]. Line a baking sheet with parchment paper.

In a medium bowl, combine the oats, pistachios, pumpkin seeds, rosemary, salt, and pepper. Fold in the egg white until all of the granola is coated. Transfer to the prepared baking sheet and spread into a single layer.

Bake until the oats begin to brown, about 15 minutes.

Remove from the oven and let cool completely. Store in an airtight container at room temperature for up to 1 week.

acknowledgments

Wyatt, thank you for your endless support and patience. Thank you for always encouraging me when I second guess myself and for always being kind and supportive when I need a helping hand, when I get the kitchen dirty over and over again, and when I move our furniture weekly to find the right light. My life would be insanity without you, and I can't thank you enough.

So much thanks to my supportive family for all they have done for me through the years that have led me to writing this book. Thank you to my mom for teaching me how to appreciate cooking for a crowd. Thank you to my dad for showing me the importance of working hard and being loyal. Thank you to Connie, my step-mother, for always encouraging me to embrace my creativity and telling me I was a writer at a young age. Thank you to Al, my stepfather, for showing me how fun it is to make a mess in the kitchen in the name of experimenting with new recipes. Thanks to Kurt, my older brother, for setting the bar high and encouraging me in his own way. Thank you to Grandma Betty for always being my number one fan. Finally, thank you to all my aunts, uncles, and cousins for following along and supporting my creative endeavors.

Thank you to Meg Thompson and Molly Reese-Lerner for believing I had a story worth telling and to Cindy Uh, my agent, for always answering my endless questions and being able to handle any curveball that came our way.

So many thanks to my editor, Sarah Billingsley, over at Chronicle for believing in this book and turning it into a reality. A big thanks to Alice Chau for designing such a gorgeous layout and everyone else behind the scenes at Chronicle who dedicated their time to making this book a success.

Thank you to my dear friend, Ella Hartley, who not only flew halfway across the country on several occasions to assist me with photographing and proofing this book but spent hundreds of hours on the phone listening and encouraging me through the entire process. Thank you to Anna Powell Teeter for assisting me on several of my shoots and Susie Tanney for always answering my texts and hand modeling for me when needed.

So much thanks to all of my recipe testers who made sure these recipes were accessible for all: Alissa Wolbers, Allyson Batis, Ann Jonker, Anna Wallace, Caroline Marchildon, Grace Poser, Leah Fithian, Kathy Cherven, Katie Grimm, Kelsey Trost-Burton, Riley Manion, Shelley Ludman, Steph Evans, Will Muir, and Sarah Nichols.

Thanks so much to Anderson Orchard in Mooresville, Indiana for letting me photograph their beautiful apple orchard. The fall chapter would not be the same without those photos.

And most importantly, thank you to all the *Vegetarian 'Ventures* blog readers for giving me an excuse to cook non-stop and share it with the world. This book could not be possible without all of you following along from whatever end of the world you reside.

index